SpringerBriefs in Economics

More information about this series at http://www.springer.com/series/8876

aj

vironmental Regulations and Innovation in Advanced Automobile Technologies

Perspectives from Germany, India, China and Brazil

Springer

Ashish Bharadwaj
Jindal Global Law School
O.P. Jindal Global University
Sonipat, Haryana
India

ISSN 2191-5504 ISSN 2191-5512 (electronic)
SpringerBriefs in Economics
ISBN 978-981-10-6951-2 ISBN 978-981-10-6952-9 (eBook)
https://doi.org/10.1007/978-981-10-6952-9

Library of Congress Control Number: 2017955260

Printed on acid-free paper

This Springer imprint is published by Springer Nature
The registered company is Springer Nature Singapore Pte Ltd.
The registered company address is: 152 Beach Road, #21-01/04 Gateway East, Singapore 189721, Singapore

Technology certainly owes an apology to ecology:
But, with synergy, it offers an opportunity to fortify recovery.

To my mother, the strongest person I know,
for her generosity

Acknowledgements

I acknowledge with gratitude the financial support I received for my research from the Max Planck Gesellschaft and the Max Planck Institute for Innovation and Competition in Munich (Germany) during 2009 and 2012; and the Institute for Innovation Research, Technology Management and Entrepreneurship (INNO-tec) at Ludwig-Maximilians-Universität München (LMU), Munich, Germany, during 2012 and 2014.

I am particularly grateful to Professor Dietmar Harhoff, an academic giant in the field of innovation economics, for providing me with the protected academic time and continuous support.

This would probably not have been possible without friends who were an integral part of my social support system. I have countless memories of spending wonderful time with Thimo, Ana, Jason Alka, and Augustiner. Mrinalini brought in the much needed positive vibe in our office room, and I am grateful to her for introducing the idea of balance at work and in personal life. I remember numerous discussions I have had with Owais, a colleague then and a dear friend now, on various topics, related to our respective work and, sometimes, completely unrelated to anything meaningful. My good friend Rahul was one of the reasons I always looked forward to going back home to unwind from work.

I am forever indebted to my mother, Vinay, who has always put my interests ahead of hers. I am always thankful to my family - Manasi, Pushpam, Gargi, and Siddharth - for being a constant source of inspiration, for their uncompromising words of wisdom and untiring words of caution. I am grateful to my partner, Richa, for her help in understanding why writing this acknowledgment is important. As with so many things, I did not appreciate them then as much as I admire them now.

Liankhankhup Guite, Joy Saini and Punkhuri Chawla helped with valuable research assistance in preparation of this manuscript. I am thankful to Nupoor Singh at Springer for her time and patience.

Contents

About the Author

Dr. Ashish Bharadwaj is Assistant Professor at the Jindal Global Law School (JGLS), O.P. Jindal Global University, and Co-Director of Jindal Initiative on Research in IP and Competition (JIRICO)—a think tank focused on frontline research on issues at the interface of high-technology innovation, patents, and competition. He is Assistant Director of the Centre for Intellectual Property and Technology Law and the founding Editor of the Law & Policy Brief. He writes extensively on the role of technology and innovation in shaping societies, licensing of standard essential patents, national IPR and innovation policies. He is an affiliated faculty at the Center for Intellectual Property Research, Maurer School of Law, Indiana University, Bloomington, USA, and a Visiting Associate Professor at the Institute for Innovation Research, Hitotsubashi University, Tokyo. He holds a Ph.D. from the Max Planck Institute for Innovation and Competition, Munich; European Master in Law and Economics from Erasmus University Rotterdam, the Netherlands, University of Hamburg, Germany, and University of Manchester, UK; Master in Economic Sciences from Madras School of Economics, Anna University; and a B.A. Honors in Economics from Delhi University.

Abbreviations

ACEA	Association des Constructeurs Européens d'Automobiles (European Automobile Manufacturers Association)
ANFAVEA	Associação Nacional dos. Fabricantes de Veículos Automotores (National Association of Automobile Manufacturers, Brazil)
ARAI	Automotive Research Association of India
BIC	Brazil, India and China
BRICS	Brazil, Russia, India, China and South Africa
BS-I	Bharat Stage Emission Norms-I
CAFE	Corporate Average Fuel Economy
CCV	Closed Crankcase Ventilation
CGPDTM	Controller General of Patents Designs and Trademarks (India)
CNG	Compressed Natural Gas
CO	Carbon monoxide
CONAMA	Conselho Nacional do Meio Ambiente (National Council for the Environment, Brazil)
CPCB	Central Pollution Control Board, India
CRDI	Common Rail Diesel Injection
DOC	Diesel oxidation catalyst
DPF	Diesel particulate filter
EEC/EC	European Economic Community/European Community
EEV	Enhanced Environmentally Friendly Vehicle
EGR	Exhaust gas recirculation
EPB	Environment Pollution Bureau, People's Republic of China
EPO	European Patent Office
GDI	Gasoline direct injection
GVW	Gross vehicle weight
HC	Hydrocarbons
IBAMA	Instituto Brasileiro do Meio Ambiente e dos Recursos Naturais Renováveis (Brazilian Institute of Environment and Renewable Natural Resources)

ICCT	International Council on Clean Transportation
ICE	Internal combustion engine
IEA	International Energy Agency
INPI	Instituto Nacional da Propriedade Industrial (National Institute of Industrial Property, Brazil)
IPC	International Patent Classification
LDVs	Light duty vehicles
LNC/LNT	Lean NOx catalyst/trap
LPG	Liquefied petroleum gas
MEP	Ministry of Environmental Protection, People's Republic of China
MHCVs	Medium and heavy commercial vehicles
MoEF	Ministry of Environment and Forests, India
MPFI	Multipoint fuel injection
NAAQS	National Ambient Air Quality Standards (USA)
NMHC	Non-methane hydrocarbons
NOx	Nitrogen oxide
OBD	Onboard diagnostics
OECD	Organization for Economic Cooperation and Development
OICA	Organisation Internationale des Constructeurs d'Automobiles (International Organization of Motor Vehicle Manufacturers)
PM	Particulate Matter
PROCONVE	Programa de Controle da Poluição do Ar por Veículos Automotores (Motor Vehicle Emission Control Program, Brazil)
RSI	Regulatory Stringency Index
SCR	Selective Catalytic Reduction
SEPA	State Environmental Protection Administration, People's Republic of China
SIAM	Society of Indian Automobile Manufacturers
SIPO	State Intellectual Property Office, People's Republic of China
SO_2	Sulfur dioxide
THC	Total hydrocarbons
UNEP	United Nations Environment Programme
UNFCCC	United Nations Framework Convention on Climate Change
USEPA	United States Environment Protection Agency
VOC	Volatile organic compounds

List of Figures

List of Tables

Chapter 1
Evolution of the Global Automobile Industry

Abstract The global automotive industry has undergone significant changes since the invention of the automobile. The industry has transformed from being dominated by the USA in the early 1900s to being divided between a variety of different countries, each with their own unique strengths and weaknesses. The underlying technology has also experienced radical technological innovations, with the increasing popularity of diesel, hybrid and fully electric vehicles helping to diversify the market. Changes in the regulatory environment and internal production processes have also molded the industry, making more efficient cars accessible to the mass public. In years to come, automotive companies in Brazil, India and China (part of the BRIC group) are likely to continue to grow their share of the global market, while concomitant rise in environmental concerns are likely to bring substantial changes in how the industry adapts and evolves in the future. This study has three broad objectives. First, to trace how regulations pertaining to vehicular pollution have changed and what factors caused them to become more stringent over time. Second, how patenting of promising environment-friendly inventions, as a result of continuous technological innovation, promises to ameliorate some environmental concens. Third, in order to relate these two phenomena, an attempt is made to understand the impact of regulatory stringency on the level of patenting of technologies that are both fuel-saving as well as emission-reducing.

1.1 From Steam and Electricity to Petrol and Diesel

This chapter presents a brief account of how the dynamic automobile industry emerged and evolved in the past two hundred years in different parts of the world. Although automobiles have been around for several decades, it was not until the invention of the combustion engine that a mass global demand for cars began to develop (McNally 2017, p. 42). Their proliferation was partly due to improvements in technology and partially enabled by advancements in the efficiency of production processes, leading to the availability of affordable vehicles. This chapter is aimed at

A. Bharadwaj, *Environmental Regulations and Innovation in Advanced Automobile Technologies*, SpringerBriefs in Economics,
https://doi.org/10.1007/978-981-10-6952-9_1

describing the way in which the industry has evolved, and the various different changes that its economic structure and customer base have undergone.

Although vehicles now are, in many ways, synonymous with the internal combustion engine, the early automobiles predated its invention by over a century and were reliant upon steam power and electricity - a technological breakthrough then and an archaic technology now. Market for steam-powered cars was initially slow to develop, as they were extremely cumbersome and heavy but, in the early nineteenth century, a modest demand for these vehicles developed in England to carry cargo and passengers (Nyamwange and Nyamwange 2014, p. 12). They started to be used in France and the U.S. , with demand being partly driven by innovations such as multi-speed, the hand brake, and a smoother steering mechanism. However, there was eventually a backlash against such vehicles, with residents complaining about them being used on public roads. Horse carriage manufacturers also protested about the adverse impact of motor vehicles on the use of horse and carts, possibly in an attempt to ward off what they perceived as being an emerging source of competition (Black 2014, p. 103). This led to the passing of the Locomotive Act 1865, which stated that self-propelling vehicles could not be used on public roads unless an accompanying pedestrian walked in front of them blowing a horn and waving a red flag (Black 2012, p. 107). This practically killed the market for the steam-powered automobile in England.

In 1876, Nicklaus Otto invented the four-stroke internal combustion engine and German engineer and designer Karl Benz incorporated it into a car shortly afterwards (Hatheway 2012, p. 176). By 1904, engineers had managed to mitigate the problems of odor, vibrations and noise, stemming from the engine of cars, which significantly boosted their popularity, making them the most widely purchased form of automobile (Saxena 2009, p. 273). The next major technological breakthrough came in 1892, when German engineer and inventor Rudolf Diesel invented the diesel engine. Diesel was cheaper and safer than petrol, providing Diesel's creation with an obvious advantage over Otto's engine. Unfortunately, since the initial design was unreliable, it did not make an impact upon the market until quite some time later, which meant that the first mass-produced car, the Model T, still used a petrol engine.

In 1896, Henry Ford produced the first Model T, which was an automobile that was specifically designed to be reasonably priced and accessible to the mass public. This marked a move away from cars being the domain of the wealthy, and an entry into the popular market. Ford believed that if his factory workers produced a greater number of cars within a smaller period of time and offered them for less money, it would be likely to generate high sales figures. He pioneered assembly line production techniques in order to reduce the cost of making the vehicles, and, by 1914, he had put a system in place that enabled workers to assemble a car within one and a half hours. By 1916, Model T cars were selling for $400 in the United States, which made them the cheapest model on the market by a considerable margin (Carbaugh 2014, p. 89).

Ford had originally intended to produce several different models but abandoned these plans due to the success of the Model T, focusing all of his efforts on it. By

1921, the Model T had a 60% share of the global automobile market. The spread of this technological marvel for use by public throughout the developed world was enabled by the dissemination of thousands of kits for local assembly and an expansive network of agents and dealerships. By the time Ford ceased production of the model in 1927, 15 million cars had been sold all over the world. The market for automobiles had also been transformed from wealthy individuals wishing to outwardly display their affluence to ordinary working- and middle-class consumers (Parissien 2013, p. 14).

Up until this point, cars had been shunned by majority of the working population and viewed as vehicles for ostentatious showmanship, especially in markets outside of Europe and the USA. The Model T was instrumental in altering this perception, and ensuring that they were popular among the masses.

1.2 The Big Three

In the 1920s, new competition emerged from General Motors and Chrysler within the U.S. to challenge the Model T's global dominance of the automobile industry (Carbaugh 2015, p. 75). General Motors conducted careful systematic market research aimed at gaining detailed insight into the sales potential within each market. The company used vehicle registration data to monitor shifts in demand, ensuring that it developed vehicles to suit the requirements of the consumer. Whereas Ford produced a single model at a low cost, General Motors sought to compete both by offering a wide variety of different automobiles, and by going to great lengths to remain abreast of the latest preferences and trends.

The constant adaptation to match cars to customers' requirements meant that General Motors had to adapt its assembly techniques so that they could be altered on a regular basis, and yet remain capable of facilitating mass production of vehicles. This involved the introduction of more flexible machines that were capable of carrying out a number of different functions. In 1920, Walter Chrysler, a manager at General Motors, announced his resignation from the company following a dispute with its founder, William Durant, and started the Chrysler Motor Corporation two years later. It soon rivaled General Motors and Ford in terms of its customer base, differentiating itself by producing a constant stream of innovative new components and accessories (Olson and Mendoza 2015, pp. 109–110). Ford, General Motors, and Chrysler became known as the "Big Three," and dominated the global market for decades to come, and ensured that the U.S. was at the forefront of the automobile industry. However, the petrol engine was soon to be joined by a brand new competitor, as diesel engine was finally about to take off.

In the 1930s, a British company, F. Perkins Ltd., developed a more efficient diesel engine (Jones 2014, p. 159). A French company, Citroen, was the first car company to take advantage of the new, improved diesel engine, incorporating it into some versions of its Rosalie model in 1934. Mercedes-Benz quickly followed suit, using a diesel engine in its 260d, which was released the following year.

One of the main catalysts for the growth of diesel's popularity thereafter was its use during the war in naval vessels, aircrafts, and other military vehicles. This helped cement its application in the public consciousness, and it started to be used more in road haulage and agricultural vehicles. In the 1950s, its use in cars increased with British manufacturers Austin, Rover, and Standard, as well as the Italian company, Fiat, offering diesel versions of some of their models. In the 1960s, the dominant Japanese manufacturer, Isuzu Bellel joined them. The growth of diesel-powered vehicles continued to rise, for the first time, by an increasing concern for energy efficiency. It was also boosted by a desire for a cheaper alternative to petrol, as prices dramatically rose following conflict in the Middle East (Long 2013, pp. 32–33).

1.3 Rise of Non-U.S. Companies

As the popularity of diesel continued to rise, so did competition against the Big Three from outside of the USA. In the 1960s, as consumers began to look elsewhere for vehicles, foreign models experienced a rapid growth in popularity, prompting Ford, General Motors, and Chrysler to criticize the government for failing to support its domestic automobile industry. The companies also attempted to hold on to their dominance in the domestic market by branding buyers who bought imported cars as unpatriotic (Klingle 2014, p. 487). Towards the start of the 1970s, skyrocketing oil prices and an increasing public awareness of environmentalism caused some consumers in the United States to gravitate towards smaller, less polluting European and Japanese automobiles (Olson and Mendoza 2015, p. 110). Up until the mid 1960s, Japanese car designs were viewed as attempts to replicate American and European models. The island nation mainly produced cars for domestic consumption, with only a very small share being exported overseas. During the late 1960s, Japanese companies began to focus more on small cars with modest engines of 360 cc or less in order to avoid tax, leading to a dramatic increase in exports. At the same time, the domestic market continued to grow, transforming Japan into a top contender within the global automobile industry (Carstea 2015, p. 279).

Toyota improved upon the flexible mass production techniques pioneered by General Motors to enable its products to be tailored to latest global trends. Its factories started creating spare parts that could be used interchangeably across different models, allowing it to aggressively promote new models at a lower cost within a short period of time (Carbaugh 2014, p. 89). Toyota also pioneered a strategy known as "just-in-time manufacturing", which involved making the right components available in the required quantity at precisely the right time they were needed, in order to minimize wastage of time and resources. It was partly enabled by cultural factors, including a strong Japanese work ethic that emerged following World War II—a strong sense of equality, and a high level of coordination and team play among Japanese employees, and the fact that work frequently took precedence over other activities in Japanese society (Lai and Cheng 2009, pp. 9–10). Honda and Nissan followed suit and adopted similar techniques, which enabled them to sell high-quality cars at a relatively low price. The "just-in-time" method has been credited as one of the main factors that reduced America's grip on the global automotive industry, and enabled Japan to take over a substantial share of the market (Shimokawa 2010, p. 2). The Japanese practice of *kaizen* was also influential in facilitating the growth of its car companies externally, and consolidating operations internally. This entailed shop-floor workers constantly attempting to enhance manufacturing processes via minor changes to their daily work. This brought to attention the idea that incremental innovation involving the entire workforce can enable continuous and sustanied improvements in technical and managerial functions.

Around mid-20th century, European manufacturers also concentrated their efforts on compact vehicles and were able to take advantage of the increasing popularity of these cars. By 1959, Germany's Volkswagen Beetle had managed to gain a tenth of the American market (Klier 2009, p. 5), and remained the nation's most popular imported vehicle until the 1970s. British and Italian companies, drawn by the sudden demand for small foreign cars, started to make in-roads outside their domestic markets and also began penetrating non-European markets.

By 1981, the hegemony of the big American automobile manufacturers was declining and the companies realized that they were simply unabe to compete globally. Meanwhile, the Japanese and German manufacturers had grown in terms of global competitiveness (Shimokawa 2010, p. 10). To respond to such crisis, Ford adopted elements of the Japanese production system and worked ceaselessly to integrate them into its factories, Chrysler was granted a government loan to avoid bankruptcy, and General Motors and Toyota engaged in a profitable joint venture called New United Motor Manufacturing Inc., which managed to save it from financial ruin (Klepper 2016, p. 107).

1.4 Tightening Environmental Regulations

Another reason for dwindling profitability of the Big Three were the strict environmental regulations that were imposed on the American automotive industry. Their origins can be traced back to the Californian environmental crisis in the mid 1960s, which saw "pollution" and "LA" become synonymous in the minds of many Americans. Consequently, the Federal Air Quality Act 1967 was enacted, which not only put minimum federal standards in place, but also stated that states were permitted to make the requirements stricter if they deemed that it was necessary to do so.

The passing of this Act drew attention to the issue of pollution, and, in 1970, the Clean Air Act was enacted, mandating the inclusion of catalytic converters in new automobiles and placing additional limitations upon harmful emissions (Ross et al. 2014, pp. 781–786). In 1975, the Energy Policy Conservation Act was brought in to set minimum fuel efficiency standards. Since then, the rules regarding fuel efficiency and emissions norms have gradually tightened, posing new challenges and creating new opportunities for car manufacturers.

In addition to additional environmental and business responsibilities, there was growing public demand for companies to place environmentalism at the forefront of their businesses.

Car companies overseas managed to get their act together around the same time. In the mid 2000s, Toyota developed a reputation as a green company due to development of its hybrid Prius model. However, in reality, the Prius only constituted 3% of its sales, with gas guzzling sports utility vehicles comprising a considerably higher proportion (Banerjee 2009, pp. 87–88). European automotive companies also took advantage of the rise of environmentalism, innovating new technologies in order to change their business model and adhere to more stringent regulatory requirements (Bailey et al. 2010, p. 315). They actively searched for means of capitalizing upon the requirement for less polluting and more efficient automobiles. The global market is now being shared among an increasingly wide range of nations, and BRIC countries are beginning to emerge as major players. The era of a small number of nations dominating the industry appears to have come to an end.

1.5 The Rise of Brazil, India, and China

In 1997, Europe, Japan, and the USA represented just over three quarters of global automobile production. This figure had declined to approximately half by 2009, partly due to increasing market share of companies in Brazil, Russia, India and China (Bailey et al. 2010, pp. 311–313). The rise of the BRIC nations' automotive industries has partly been facilitated by the growing per capita incomes, sustained improvement in road infrastructure and mass production of all types of vehicles. Some of the established car brands are now under the ownership of firms in emerging economies, for example the Jaguar Land Rover was acquired by Indian manufacturer Tata, and Volvo is owned by Chinese company Geely.

China has experienced a particularly substantial growth in its share of the global automobile market, rising from 3% in 1997 to 22% in 2009 (Bailey et al. 2010, pp. 311), making it the world's largest car manufacturing country (International Monetary Institute 2014, p. 114). Chinese car companies are developing the capacity to undertake complex R&D and assembly functions, and they are likely to become an even more formidable force in the years to come.

Brazil's automotive industry has also experienced a rapid spurt of growth. It is now the seventh biggest in the world (International Monetary Institute 2014, p. 114), responsible for almost a fifth of the nation's GDP. Brazil's automobile industry was in a poor state until the 1990s, with foreign firms dominating its domestic market. In an attempt to nurture a homegrown industry, industry representatives and union leaders actively helped the government, and it was agreed that the price of vehicles that they produced should be reduced, export promotion policies should be implemented, and there should be an increase in investment in

Brazilian factories aimed at modernizing production techniques. These measures enhanced productivity and brought the quality of the country's automobiles up to a globally competitive standard.

The growth of India's automotive industry, on the other hand, was stimulated by the introduction of a number of government-led initiatives since 1990s, with the recent Automotive Mission Plan in 2016 aiming to actively promote vehicle exports. Although its domestic passenger car market is still dominated by Japanese companies, homegrown automobile firms have captured 60% share of the market for commercial vehicles. Indian automotive companies also export cars to a total of 95 different countries (Sasuga 2011, p. 289).

In addition to new key players entering the global automobile industry, the other major development in recent years is the resurgence of the popularity of the electric car.

1.6 Conclusion

In the past five decades, laws pertaining to the enviornment in the United States have strived to achieve a delicate balance between the enforcement ability of different states to curb pollution, and the national framework designed to meet minimum standards. The US Clean Air Act, as a federal mechanism, set the minimum benchmark for environmental regulations nationally in light of growing concerns about worsening air quality and overall impact on the ecosystem due to growth of industrial sectors, including the automobile industry. However, the individual states have discretionary powers in deciding how they will comply with this minimum threshold and they have no legal obligations to implement tighter regulations beyond the federally implemented levels. The National Ambient Air Quality Standards (NAAQS) explain this cooperative federalism framework well, where the limit of concentration of air pollutants are determined at the federal level but it is left to the states to decide how exactly they will meet this requirememt. The global automotive industry has undergone a plethora of changes since its inception. In the last three hundred years of its evolution and growth, the dominant forces within the market have become increasingly more diversified, with a range of different actors now vying for control of the industry. Environmental concerns resulting in the rise of unconventional transport technologies have helped shape the market. Technological innovation has been the key to unlock the immense potential of the automobile industry as a way to not only ensure enhanced mobility for users but also in adaptation efforts towards improving our air quality, and mitigating the deleterious effect the industry has had so far. In this context, patents have been an extremely useful, albeit imperfect, measure of innovation vitality. They help researchers assess the capability of the overall industry to adjust to old and new regulations and, in turn, complement the regulatory agencies in framing the right regulations and laws. The cries and alarms about the imminent death of the ICE technology that changed the world have grown in the last few years. Similar to the concerns expressed by stakeholders in the horse carriage industry a century ago, the 'perennial gale' of creative destruction are moving in favour of new and improved technologies for transport. Climate change and energy security concerns are compelling governments to provide incentives for investments in clean energy sources and cleaner ways to run energy-intensive products and industries. Electric mobility is indeed the future of mobility but there are still several technical and non-technical challenges it faces, and it is unlikely to fully replace the conventional combustion technologies, on a global scale, any time soon. Riding on the back of universal electrification, Europe was the first to present the world a real possibility of a move away from the mightiest combustion technology in history, towards newer modes of transport, including hybrid and fully electric. Not only are manufacturers in Europe (led by the German giants of the automobile industry) changing the long term outlook of their business in favour of electric mobility, the lawmakers are keen to send the right message of where they wish to see their societies move in the future. It is crucial to take a step back to understand how innovation changed the scope and impact of the industry in the last few decades, and how regulations played a role in this, which is the focus of this book. The following chapters of this book present several aspects of the automobile industry, including its progression in conjunction with growth of economies, impact on the human and physical environment, response of innovators that have been leading the growth trajectory of this industry, as well as response of national governments to the looming environmental crises. Chapter 2 presents an overview of some major global developments in the form of cumulative innovation of new automobile technologies that took place in the previous decade in major parts of the world. This chapter also presents theoretical ideas, along with empirical evidence, that have emerged from the academic literature around environmental regualtion, innovation and economic growth. Chapter 3 consolidates review of some major scholarly work covering three major facets of environmental regulations - economic growth, technological innovation and industrial competitiveness. Chapter 4 brings forth various instruments of environmental regulation, followed by a compilation of environmental legislations and development of standards that are relevant to the automobile industry of Germany, India, China and Brazil. Chapter 5 explores the technical aspects of environment friendly technologies (within the conventional powertrain and ICE mechanism) that have the potential to mitigate the challenges posed by vehicular pollution and high fuel consumption. This chapter also introduces the method by which the International Patent Classification system has been used in this study, and finally presents a novel regulatory stringency index that has been developed for the four countries mentioned above. Building on the work in the previous chapter, Chapter 6 introduces different characteristics of patent data that has been used in this study. This chapter throws light on patenting trends across relevant technologies during the period 1985 till 2011 in Germany, India, China and Brazil. Chapter 7 presents the empirical methodology used in investigating the impact of regulatory stringency across the four countries on patenting (as a measure of technological innovation in this industry), followed by key findings that have emerged. Finally, Chapter 8 presents managerial and public policy implications on the basis of the findings of this study.

References

Bailey, D., De Ruyter, A., Michie, J., & Tyler, P. (2010). Global restructuring and the auto industry. *Cambridge Journal of Regions, Economy and Society, 3*(3), 311–318.

Banerjee, S. (2009). *Corporate social responsibility*. Cheltenham, UK: Edward Elgar Publishing.

Black, B. (2012). *Crude reality: Petroleum in world history*. Plymouth, UK: Rowman & Littlefield Publishers.

Black, B. (2014). Automobile history. In B. Black, D. Hassenzahl, J. Stephens, G. Weisel, & N. Gift (Eds.), *Climate change* (Vol. 1, pp. 102–118). Santa Barbara, CA: ABC-Clio.

Burton, N. (2013). *A history of electric cars*. Marlborough, UK: Crowood Press.

Carbaugh, R. (2014). *Contemporary economics*. Abingdon, UK: Routledge.

Carbaugh, R. (2015). *International economics*. Boston, MA: Cengage Learning.

Carstea, V. (2015). Delocalizing the Japanese automotive industry and the Romanian market. *Romanian Economic and Business Review, 10*(4), 278–283.

Hatheway, A. (2012). *Remediation of former manufactured gas plants and other coal-tar sites*. Boca Raton, FL: CRC Press.

International Monetary Institute. (2014). *The internationalization of the renminbi*. Abingdon, UK: Routledge.

Jones, B. (2014). *The Peterborough book of days*. Stroud, UK: The History Press.

Klepper, S. (2016). *Experimental capitalism*. Woodstock: Princeton University Press.

Klier, T. (2009). From tail fins to hybrids: How Detroit lost its dominance of the U.S. auto market. *Economic Perspectives, 2*(33), 2–17.

Klingle, M. (2014). The nature of desire: Consumption in environmental history. In A. Isenberg (Ed.), *The oxford handbook of environmental history* (pp. 467–521). Oxford, UK: Oxford University Press.

Lai, K., & Cheng, T. (2009). *Just-in-time logistics*. Farnham, UK: Gower Publishing.

Long, B. (2013). *The zero carbon car*. Marlborough, UK: Crowood Press.

McNally, R. (2017). *Crude volatility*. New York, NY: Columbia University Press.

Miller, P., & Solomon, M. (2009, June). A brief history of technology-forcing motor vehicle regulations. *EM*, 4–8.

Myopi, R. (2012). The impact of the "BRIC Thesis" and the rise of emerging economies on global competitive advantage: Will there be a shift from West to East? *Journal of Applied Business and Economics, 13*(3), 36–47.

Nyamwange, J., & Nyamwange, D. (2014). Major innovations in transportation: Evolution of automobiles. *International Journal of Humanities and Social Science, 4*(5), 11–16.

Olson, J., & Mendoza, A. (2015). *American economic history*. Santa Barbara, CA: Greenwood.

Parissien, S. (2013). *The life of the automobile*. London: Atlantic Books.

Peterson, S., & Michalek, J. (2013). Cost-effectiveness of plug-in hybrid electric vehicle battery capacity and charging infrastructure investment for reducing US gasoline consumption. *Energy Policy, 52,* 429–438.

Ross, K., Chmiel, J., & Ferkol, T. (2014). The impact of the clean air act. *Journal of Pediatrics, 161*(5), 781–786.

Sasuga, K. (2011). The Impact of the Rise of Chinese and Indian automobile industries. In P. Macha & T. Drobik (Eds.), *The scale of globalization. Think globally, act locally, change individually in the 21st century* (pp. 286–291). Ostrava, Czech Republic: University of Ostrava.

Saxena, S. (2009). *Automobile engineering*. New Delhi, India: University Science Press.

Shimokawa, K. (2010). *Japan and the global automotive industry*. Cambridge, UK: Cambridge University Press.

Chapter 2
Changing Dynamics of the Industry

Abstract An overview of the global automotive industry and how it is inextricably linked with growth of economies is presented in this chapter. For several developed economies, the automobile industry has been a driver of economic growth, contributing significantly to GDP and to the exchequer. Nowadays, conventional engines are remarkably cleaner and more powerful than their counterparts from a few decades ago. Several important technologies are responsible for this paradigm shift in internal combustion engine technology from lowly carburetors to efficient fuel injectors to precise (gasoline) direct injectors, from heavy iron to lighter aluminum, from multivalve to enhanced variable valve timing, from overhead valve to improved overhead camshafts and finally the advancements in the embedded computer systems, engine controls units and onboard diagnostics to optimize overall performance. This chapter also throws light on the environmental challenges the industry poses, and its responsibilities in tackling these challenges.

2.1 The Automotive Industry and Economic Growth

For several developed economies, the automobile industry has been a driver of economic growth, contributing significantly to GDP and to the exchequer. With huge investments being pumped into the automobile sector, the focus is shifting yet again to low emission and high fuel efficiency in automobiles. The production is increasingly shifting to emerging markets such as China, India, and Brazil. The financial crises may reinforce, and even accelerate, this shift in favor of the emerging economies. The five members of the BRICS group (Brazil, Russia, India, China, and South Africa) were largely responsible for the (albeit modest) growth in world GDP in the aftermath of the 2008–09 global financial crises.

Currently, even with relatively smaller real incomes in these emerging economies, the average cost of purchasing and running a car is drastically higher than in

This chapter contains some portions from a previous publication: Bharadwaj, A (2015). 'Technological and Socio-Economic Issues in the Global Automobile Industry', Transp. in Dev. Econ. 1: 33. https://doi.org/10.1007/s40890-015-0005-2

A. Bharadwaj, *Environmental Regulations and Innovation in Advanced Automobile Technologies*, SpringerBriefs in Economics,
https://doi.org/10.1007/978-981-10-6952-9_2

industrialized economies. According to IMF data analyzed by the Economist Intelligence Unit, Shanghai, Sao Paolo and New Delhi surpass London, Berlin, Tokyo and New York in terms of average cost of owning a car.[1] Nevertheless, car makers are flocking to emerging markets, in an attempt to exploit the growing demand and to counter rising taxes on foreign made vehicles. It was recently reported that the German automobile giant *Daimler* plans to setup a new assembly plant in Brazil to roll out its new C Class from 2015.[2] Other German manufacturers such as *BMW* and *Audi* have also announced plans to set up or expand plants in the coming year to gain market share in Brazil, which is dominated by Fiat, Volkswagen, GM, and Ford. Similarly, in India, Daimler is investing more in its existing plant in Pune and in order to attract less import duties, started assembling new E Class in this plant from 2013. The small and medium scale ancillary industrial units concomitantly move with the big manufacturers to new markets and collectively contribute to value addition, employment generation, and technology diffusion in the local economy of the host country.

USA, Germany, and Japan have been the technology pioneers in automobile engineering and sales for several decades now. Between 2000 and 2007, the share of the United States and Japan in global production fell from 40% to 30%, while the share of the non-OECD countries increased from production of one in ten cars to one in five cars (OECD 2009a, 2009b). The growing demand in different geographical regions has led to an increase in the minimum efficient scale of production of most automobile manufacturers. One consequence is an increase in the number of mergers and acquisitions, as well as collaborations in the industry to take advantage of the economies of scale and scope. The financial crises during the last decade put enormous strain on the global transport industry because of plummeting car sales, tighter access to credit, and higher input cost across countries for several successive periods. According to European Automobile Manufacturers' Association (ACEA), the decline in demand for new cars in 2012 in the EU was at a historic low since 1990. Four years earlier, General Motors had filed for one of the largest bankruptcies in the history of corporate America. This led to an array of stimulus packages and corporate reorganizations putting additional financial stress on the global economy.

Therefore, the currently distressed global car manufacturers seem to be counting on the ongoing sales surge in Asian economies, as well as on America's automotive market, which is now in a recovery mode. To maintain its competitive advantage in

---

[1]Of the two components of ownership cost, purchase price and cost of running the vehicle, the former was almost three times higher in the emerging economies and the average cost ranged from approximately $90,000 to $120,000. The cost is for buying a typical family car with a 1.8–2.5L engine in 2010. The running cost includes road tax, registration-fee, service, insurance, and petrol consumption for 10,000 miles (16,100 km) at 35 mpg (12.4 km/L) for three years.

[2]Reuters via the German weekly Der Spiegel revealed this in August 2013. It should be noted that Mercedes was manufacturing the A Class hatchback since 1999 at the Juiz de Fora plant but since the plant was retooled for production of commercial trucks, production of passenger car ended in 2010.

low-emissions engine technology, Europe has repeatedly given signals to car manufactures that they will have to adhere to fuel efficiency and emission targets by 2025. The European Parliament's Environment Committee confirmed the proposed limit of 95 g of carbon dioxide per kilometer for 2020, which implies that the average car should require approximately 4 litres of fuel for a driving range of 100 km. Further, it was decided that emissions should be brought down to 68–78 g per kilometer at a mileage of 100 km in 3 litres by 2025.

2.2 Innovation in the Automotive Industry

The 2009 UNFCCC meeting in Bonn brought the issue of the role of (clean) technology in reducing emissions at the center stage of intellectual property discussions. The Rio summit held in June 2012 focused on two central themes—green economy and the institutional framework for sustainable development. For the first time, there was a heated debate between two polarized environmental groups over intellectual property, and, specifically, on patent law and technology transfer. The argument put forth was that patents are primarily responsible for the high cost of such low-carbon technologies. The developed countries, on the other hand, argue that patents are a good way to incentivize innovation in clean technologies and weak intellectual property regimes are responsible for the slow rate of transfer of such technologies (Barton 2007).

The current internal combustion technology, building on the technological innovations of the past 100 years, is considered by many to be ahead of the electric propulsion technology. The gas-electric hybrids, which are touted as the transition technology to the fully electric car also burn fuel in their engines. Consumer skepticism about the driving range of electric passenger cars (*range anxiety*) continues to prevail. Further, the existing fuel cell and battery technologies are tractors and long-haul trailers, unless there is a revolutionary technological breakthrough soon.[3] This can partly explain why, despite all media hype, billions in government subsidies and increasing number of car models, the market for battery-powered vehicles has not taken off. However, the shale gas boom in natural gas in USA is expected to favor the commercial vehicle segment, which is the backbone of the inter-state transport of several goods throughout the country.

Realizing the slow progress of battery technology for MHCVs, *Cummins*, a big automotive engine manufacturer, recently introduced heavy engines that run on liquefied natural gas which is an alternate fuel having a lower price and smaller carbon footprint.[4] Compressed natural gas, on the other hand, has a reduced energy density that limits range of vehicles and increases refueling frequency. It is

[3]The promising rechargeable non-aqueous lithium-air battery, being developed by researchers at the University of St. Andrews, is receiving a great deal of interest.

[4]The bulk of demand for such heavy commercial vehicles comes from big shippers in the FMCG and logistics industry (such as Procter & Gamble, United Parcel Services, FedEx, Walmart) that want to reduce reliance on transport fuel as well as earn green credentials.

favorable to vehicles that travel shorter distances such as shuttle/transit buses, garbage haulers, and small delivery vans. Government support in the form of federal and state tax concessions and grants for installation of natural gas stations has also helped with the transition to non-conventional fuels. The Global Innovation Index 2013 states that despite the economic crisis, innovation is alive and well. R&D spending levels are surpassing 2008 levels in most countries and successful local hubs are thriving. A group of dynamic middle- and low-income countries including China, Costa Rica, India, and Senegal—are outpacing their peers, but have not broken into the top of the rankings.

2.3 New Technology and Related Issues

Nowadays, conventional engines are remarkably cleaner and more powerful than their counterparts from a few decades ago. Several important technologies are responsible for this paradigm shift in internal combustion engine technology from lowly carburetors to efficient fuel injectors to precise (gasoline) direct injectors, from heavy iron to lighter aluminum, from multivalve to enhanced variable valve timing, from overhead valve to improved overhead camshafts and finally the advancements in the embedded computer systems, engine controls units and onboard diagnostics to optimize overall performance. There is a virtual consensus among automotive engineers that a diesel-turbo engine delivers a greater torque surge and better mileage relative to a comparable petrol counterpart in standard driving conditions.[5] But, a huge drawback is the difficulty in controlling smog-and acid rain-causing nitrogen oxide (NO_x) emissions in a diesel vehicle. Diesel engines are also relatively more expensive to develop due to the hardware (such as turbo-booster components and intricate injection systems) that runs the complex diesel combustion process. It should be noted that two factors make diesel preferable to petrol in European countries. First, higher cetane rating that makes it relatively easier to curtail NO_x emissions, and second, NO_x limits are generally stricter in USA than in Europe. In order to meet these stricter limits, manufacturers in USA are compelled to incorporate expensive after-treatment equipment to decrease tailpipe (PM) emissions. Such after-treatment devices fitted onboard diesel vehicles make them even more expensive.

The negative perception of diesel prevailed in India for a long time. Overloaded public transport buses, aged passenger vehicles, and under maintained commercial vehicles—all running on diesel and emitting noxious fumes were the most visible on Indian roads and, consequently, became synonymous with the dirty fuel.[6] This perception has undergone a change in the last few years in which the advances in

[5]Diesel is inherently a more combustible fuel at high pressures than gasoline, which is a reason why diesel engines do not require spark plugs.

[6]Reasons for such negative views are the higher noise and vibration levels owing to the more explosive diesel combustion process.

diesel engine technologies have made the diesel-run cars not only more fuel efficient and cheaper to run,[7] but also less expensive to maintain than their petrol counterparts. After the introduction of stricter emission norms in India (such as BS III and IV) with reduced sulfur content to 50 ppm, diesel has indeed become a cleaner fuel.[8] China initially scheduled the nationwide implementation of China IV diesel standard (similar to Euro IV) in January 2011 but later postponed it until July 2013.

2.4 Recent Developments

An indicator of car manufacturers' response to stricter fuel economy and emission standards is the changing trend of vehicular length and weight. Despite increasing fuel efficiency and tighter emissions standards, installation of safety devices and infotainment systems, long running car brands such as the *Volkswagen Golf Series* and *Peugeot20 Series* were, for the first time, downsized in both length and weight.[9] At a time when several manufacturers such as Nissan, GM, VW's Audi, and Toyota are cutting down their electric car plans or offering lower prices to spur sales in line with current market trend, *BMW* is launching brand i3, its first all-electric hatchback. Some other relatively recent entrants in the 'non-conventional' segment were *VW's* "e-Co-Motion" concept and the "XL1" (acclaimed as a superefficient vehicle), *Land Rover's* "Electric Defender" concept car, and *Volvo's* "V60D6" plug-in diesel electric hybrid.

Substantial progress has been made in hybrid and electric vehicle technologies in the last decade, but the infrastructure required for these vehicles is still shaping up. Installation of sufficient number of charging stations is an overwhelming task and solving the problem of *range anxiety* (how far the vehicle can go with one charge) require changes in consumer perception and driving habits. On the one hand, there is the success story of *Tesla Motors* but, on the other hand, there are the recent successive bankruptcy filings by American companies in the electric propulsion segment such as Frisker Automotive, Coda Automotive, Better Place, and A123 Systems. In Europe, the latest figures from ACEA for registrations in the first quarter of 2013 show that European car sales saw a positive growth for the first time in 19 months mainly due to increased consumer confidence in German markets. *Daimler*, *Volkswagen,* and *Renault* saw the biggest increase of 11%, 9.7%,

[7]This is, in part, due to the subsidization of diesel, mainly for agricultural use, because of which there still exists an artificially created price differential between the two fuels in India.

[8]It should be noted that the allowed sulfur content internationally is 10 ppm.

[9]Heavy subsidization of fuel consumption is not considered to be efficient due to a number of reasons (1) deteriorates budget and trade deficits, (2) misallocation of public funds to these subsidies instead of social sectors, (3) volatility of crude oil price affects fiscal planning, (4) subsidies encourage consumers to buy vehicles which further adds pressure on roads and contributes to air pollution, (5) discourages investment in clean vehicle technologies.

and 5%, respectively (ACEA 2013). *Toyota Motors*, which has sold 5 million hybrid vehicles since the first *Prius* rolled out in the USA in July 2000 certainly stands out in the electric hybrid segment. With a global fleet of 20 hybrid vehicles and research collaboration with the US Department of Energy and National Renewable Energy Laboratory, Toyota now sells electric hybrid vehicles in 80 countries around the world.

2.5 Environmental Regulation and Innovation

The scholarship on environmental regulation and innovation has two specific historical strands of economic literature that are worth mentioning. First, Josef Schumpeter's seminal 1934 theoretical treatise deserves credit for the conceptualization of the idea that innovation by firms (who he called "entrepreneurs") is in response to economic constrictions they face.[10] In 1937, he wrote,

> *(It is the belief that)* economic life is essentially passive *(and)* the theory of a stationary process constitutes really the whole of theoretical economics (…) felt very strongly that this was wrong, and that there was a source of energy *(innovation)* within the economic system which would of itself disrupt any equilibrium that might be attained *(emphasis added)*

Second, Sir John Hicks gave an early hint on the concept of "induced innovation" in his famous 1932 work in which he wrote:

> a change in the relative prices of the factors of production is itself a spur to invention, and to invention of a particular kind and directed to economizing the use of a factor which has become relatively expensive.

The Porter Hypothesis suggests ways by which stricter environmental regulation within a country can increase efficiency and induce innovation resulting in (net) cost reduction and an improved competitiveness for domestic industries (Porter 1991; Porter and van der Linde 1995).

According to the "weak" version of the Porter hypothesis, carefully drafted environmental policies may increase innovation efforts. In the short run (static version), environmental regulation imposes or increases abatement and compliance costs for a firm diverting funds away from production and investment leading to slower aggregate economic growth. The inward movement in Fig. 2.1a illustrates this.[11] But, the long-run effect (Fig. 2.1b) of the regulation is to improve the

---

[10]This stems from his work "The Theory of Economic Development" which was published in German in 1912 and was revised in English in 1934. His later works, especially "Capitalism, Socialism and Democracy" in 1942 extended this argument based on R&D activities in large scale firms.

[11]This graphical analysis is adapted from De Canio (1997) and Swanson (2008). A Production Possibility Frontier (PPF) shows how an economy uses its resource endowments to produce a combination of goods. In this case, Good A is the emission-intensive good (e.g., Vehicles) and Good B does not cause emissions or minimal compared to Good A (e.g., Retail services).

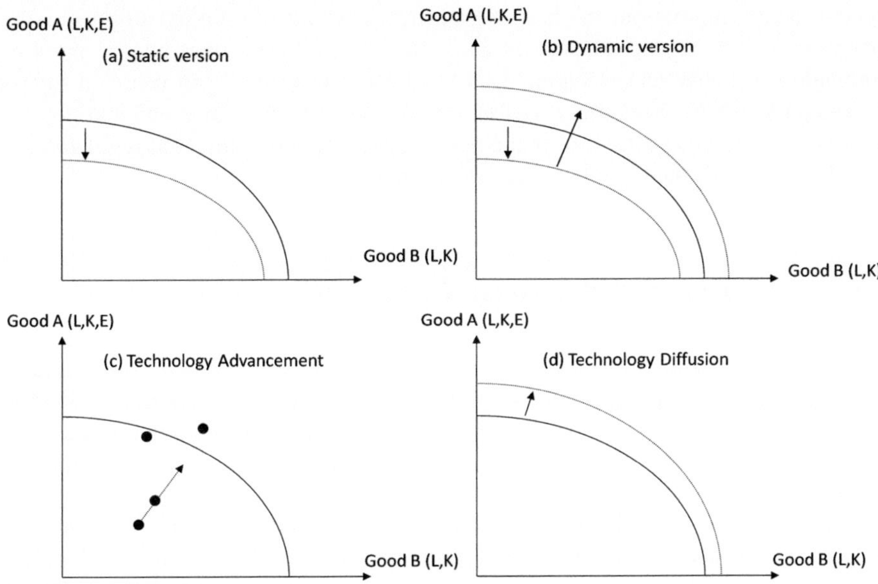

Fig. 2.1 Impact of environmental regulation: PPF analysis

ambient environment quality thereby reducing the firm's marginal cost of abatement through the following channels: (1) it acts as a signal to firms regarding future resource scarcities and technological improvements, (2) regulation addresses the uncertainty underlying the viability of potential environment-related investments that may lead to more innovative activities and, (3) provides opportunities to all players by "leveling the playing field" in order to solve environmental problems. The aggregate effect can go in either direction but, according to the Porter hypothesis, the net impact will be positive if the regulation is carefully drafted to incentivize firms to become more efficient. This link between stricter regulations and increase in firm performance (productivity, skilled labor, and competition) through increase in innovation and environmental quality relate to the "strong" version of the Porter Hypothesis.

For example, the 1995 catalytic converter regulation in India, introduced to curb NO_x emissions, initially proved costly for firms who had to get licenses from either the foreign innovator firms from Japan and USA or the early adopter firms from Germany. But over time it created incentives for innovation by Indian component manufacturers that were beginning to get more competitive. Figure 2.1c suggests the existence of less efficient (marginal local firms within the PPF) as well as more efficient firms (major local firms or foreign subsidiaries closer to the frontier and major foreign firms placed on or even beyond the PPF). As a result of an environmental regulation, the less efficient firms would rely on existing technologies to make the needed adjustment while the more efficient ones may respond by innovating in better technologies. This "induced innovation" can result in further expansion of PPF. Technology adoption (created by the more efficient foreign firms) can be an alternative mechanism to respond to environmental regulation, as was the case with the catalytic converter technology.

2.5.1 Theoretical and Empirical Evidence

The Porter Hypothesis, although often cited in the management and business economics literature, is based on anecdotal evidence relying on several case studies. It lacked a strong empirical grounding for a long time until researchers started to give empirical scrutiny to the causal relationship between environmental regulation and innovation.

In the automobile industry, Atkinson and Garner (1987) found that environmental regulations in the USA had a distinctly positive impact on the domestic automobile industry. In a theoretical framework, they study the regulations implemented in the USA between 1960 and 1980 including Corporate Average Fuel Economy (CAFE) standards, emission norms, and the 1963 Clean Air Act. Their conclusion was that increased competition from Japanese automakers resulted in implementation of a variety of disruptive environmental regulation in the USA, which consequently led to decline in emissions and increase in profitability for the innovating firms.[12] They cite an interesting statement by Charles Heinen, Director of Vehicle Emissions at *Chrysler*:

> Much as I hate to admit it, the EPA (United States Environment Protection Agency) accelerated the pace at which we study combustion. The knowledge we've gained is important, whether applied to emission control or fuel economy. (p. 364)

The study by Pilkington and Dyerson (2006) explored the development of the electric vehicle industry in the USA. They use 268 US patents in the electric propulsion technology class since 1976 as a means of examining technological development and analyze the impact of emission standards. They find that emission standards encouraged incremental innovation in the conventional vehicle technologies (such as the internal combustion engine) but did not encourage innovation in the non-conventional electric vehicle technologies. They use a simplified content analysis based on case studies and very basic patent count indicators for the handful of automobile companies active in the electric vehicle category. Their conclusion is

[12]The authors have emphasized that the achievement of the industry was linked with the nature of the industry and the wave of transformations that it was experiencing at that time. For the first time, the industry witnessed increased international competition and demand surge for automobiles.

that "emission reduction regulations have had a major influence in forcing the vehicle industry to develop or look for suitable alternative technologies" (p. 89).

Newell et al. (1999) generalized the Hicksian notion of inducement to investigate whether government regulations (National Appliance Energy Conservation Act, NAECA of 1987) had affected energy-efficiency innovation by formalizing the inducement hypothesis.[13] They find evidence of regulations improving energy efficiency of the consumer appliances considered in the study. They state that "both energy prices and government regulations have affected the energy efficiency of the model so from air conditioners, central air conditioners, and gas water heaters available on the market over the last four decades, although there have also been substantial improvements in energy efficiency that do not appear to be induced by price changes or regulations" (p. 31).

The literature on induced innovation in a developing country's context is scarce. Furthermore, the empirical induced innovation literature has largely treated domestic firms as homogeneous in terms of their technological capabilities. According to Rosenbaum (2002), firms with similar (observed) characteristics tend to have similar efficiency level. Conversely, differences in technological characteristics between firms result in differences in efficiency level. Aghion et al. (2004), applying technology frontier analysis in a Schumpeterian model, explain that the firms' motivation to innovate is dependent not just upon post-innovation rents but also on their level of (technological) efficiency. The "strong" version of Porter Hypothesis suggests that competition is higher as a result of a tighter (and well-crafted) regulation, which may provide incentives to innovate. However, Aghion et al. (2004) argued that innovation spurred by increased competition is expected from firms with highest efficiency (closest to the frontier) while it discourages innovation by the inefficient firms that are far within the frontier.[14]

According to Blind (2012), even though there exists a plethora of studies (based on data and anecdotal evidence) on regulations and various kinds of impacts on innovation, only recently scholars have shown interest in understanding the effect of regulation on the ability of firms to innovate. He states, "(…) these studies still provide no clear picture of whether the negative impacts of regulation outweigh the positive effects" (p. 3).

---

[13]Before them, Binswanger and Ruttan (1978) provided the first complete evaluation of the induced innovation hypothesis. Using transformation frontier (or innovation possibilities frontier) analysis, they confirmed an inducement effect in the agricultural sector. Till the 1990s almost the entire body of induced innovation literature saw the link through the lens of a macroeconomic (aggregate) production function framework. But, innovation and technological change is inherently a microeconomic (product-level) phenomenon as pointed out by Newell et al. (1999).

[14]Typically difference in efficiency between firms in an industry across countries is measured using the Mahalanobis distance where larger the distance value, further the less efficient (domestic) firm is from the benchmark firm within the technology frontier.

2.6 Overview of Green Automotive Technology

In order to comply with stricter emission regulations, emission control and fuel saving technologies are being developed to address each pollutant individually. Normally, an automotive engine does not generate a completely perfect combustion process and ends up emitting several pollutants. Major pollutants are emitted as a result of a typical engine combustion, which is then dealt differently by technologies with the aim of reducing those emissions and/or increasing fuel efficiency. For example, nitrogen oxides (NO_x) result from the reaction of nitrogen and oxygen atoms in the combustion process. Like HCs, they are precursors to the formation of ozone and contribute to formation of acid rain. Carbon monoxide (CO) occurs from incomplete combustion when the combustion fuel is not fully oxidized into carbon dioxide. Carbon dioxide, though results from complete combustion, is a classic heat-trapping greenhouse gas, which has huge potential for global warming. Needless to mention, all these pollutants can cause severe harms to human and animal health.

Some of the most relevant technologies for the IC Engine to reduce HC, CO, NO_x emissions include the catalyst technologies such as (1) substrate and coating technologies, (2) Three-way catalysts, (3) oxidization catalysts. Out of these, the NO_x control technologies have received a great deal of attention due to the increase in use of diesel-run vehicles and the potentially harmful effects of its emission are left uncontrolled. Technologies that are capable of reducing PM emissions are (1) Wall-flow filters, (2) Partial-flow filters, (3) Open-filters. According to Johnson (2009), the field of diesel engines and emission control technology has been very dynamic since the mid-1990s. Much of the technology evolution is regulatory-driven, and those regulations are now in various stages of implementation (p. 1).

Lean NO_x catalysts (LNCs) can be installed without substantial engine modifications and are capable of reducing NO_x by utilizing exhaust HCs. LNTs, on the other hand, achieve the same result more efficiently by trapping the nitrous emission and using the vehicle's fuel injection system to regenerate the trapped gas and emit the pollutant. SCR, as mentioned above, uses urea as a reducing agent to reduce NO_x, HC, and PM emissions. This technology is available in almost all Euro IV and V compliant heavy vehicles in Europe (MECA 2007).

Gasoline-powered vehicle technologies include multiple valves, variable valve timing and lift systems, gasoline direct injection, variable swept volume, downsizing of the engine, supercharging among others. Nowadays, all gasoline-run vehicles are configured with four-valves in each cylinder. In such a configuration, the overhead camshaft allows for better control of valve timings, fuel mix, and centralized placement of the spark plug for rapid combustion resulting in higher fuel efficiency. Jayat et al. (2011) investigated the Selective Catalytic Reduction (SCR) technology and its newly developed derivative (SCRi) for reduction of NO_x and PM emissions from diesel engines. They opine that this technology has the potential to enable future emission control, especially for new regulations in India.

References

ACEA. (2013). *The Automobile Industry Pocket Guide 2010, Communication Department.* Brussels: European Automobile Manufacturers Association.

Aghion, P., Bloom, N., Blundell, R., Griffith, R., & Howitt, P. (2004). Competition and innovation: An inverted-U relationship? UCL Working Paper No. 04/06, July 2004.

Atkinson, R. D., & Garner, L. (1987). Regulation as industrial policy: A case study of the U.S. auto industry. *Economic Development Quarterly, 1*(4), 358–373.

Barton, J. (2007). Intellectual property and access to clean energy technologies in developing countries an analysis of solar photovoltaic, bio fuel and wind technologies. Trade and Sustainable Energy Series, Issue Paper 2, ICTSD.

Binswanger, H. & Ruttan V. (1978). Induced Innovation - Technology, Institutions, and Development, Johns Hopkins University Press, Baltimore.

Blind, K. (2012). The impact of regulation on innovation: Compendium of evidence on the effectiveness of innovation policy intervention. Manchester Institute of Innovation Research, Manchester Business School, University of Manchester.

Decanio, S.J. (1997). Economic Modelling and the false tradeoff between environmental protection and economic growth. *Contemporary Economic Policy 15* (4):10-27

Jayat, F., Reck, A., & Babu, K. (2011). SCR and SCRi as after-treatment systems for low CO_2 and Low NO_x vehicles. SAE Technical Paper 2011-26-0038.

Johnson, T. (2009). Diesel emission control in review. *SAE International Journal of Fuels and Lubricants, 2*(1), 1–12.

MECA. (2007). Emission control technologies for diesel-powered vehicles, manufacturers of emission controls association paper, December 2007, Washington, D.C.

Newell, R. G., Jaffe, A. B., & Stavins, R. N. (1999). The induced innovation hypothesis and energy-saving technological change. *The Quarterly Journal of Economics, 114*(3), 941–975.

OECD. (2009a). Responding to the economic crisis: Fostering industrial restructuring and renewal. Paris: OECD Publishing.

OECD. (2009b). Effects of environmental policy on the type of innovation: The case of automotive emission-control technologies. In I. Hascic, F. de Vries, N. Johnstone, & N. Medhi, OECD Journal: Economic Studies, Vol. 2009.

Pilkington, A., & Dyerson, R. (2006). Innovation in disruptive regulatory environment: A patent study of electric vehicle technology development. *European Journal of Innovation Management, 9*(1), 79–91.

Porter, M. E. (1991). Americas green strategy. *Scientific American, 264*(4), 168.

Porter, M. E., & van der Linde, C. (1995). Green and competitive: Ending the stalemate. *Harvard Business Review*, September 1.

Rosenbaum, P. R. (2002). *Observational studies*. New York: Springer.

Swanson, T. (2008). Economic Growth and Environmental Regulation: A Discussion of International Experiences, Paper presented at an ADB Workshop on ‘A Macro-environmental strategy for China’ on 19 October 2008.

Chapter 3
Environment, Health, and New Technologies

Abstract This chapter presents a comprehensive review of the literature covering various facets of environmental regulations. The multidimensional association of environmental regulation with economic growth, innovation, and industrial competitiveness are laid down. The cost of regulation is considered as a major reason for the decline in industrial production. This is not only due to the institutional cost of regulation but also because of the cost imposed on firms as a result of restricted resource use. The results of studies investigating the Porter hypothesis are balanced almost equally on both sides of the inconclusive induced innovation debate. The innovation economics literature still has not gained ground in studying innovation activity, particularly environmental innovation, in developing countries. Lack of reliable, comprehensive, and accessible macroeconomic and innovation related studies was certainly one of the reasons few years ago. With the emergence of India, China, and Brazil as new economic powerhouses, new variants of policy-making, governance, and regulatory intervention are surfacing. This section attempts to bring focus on the neglected but critical issue of environmental regulation and innovation in economies, which are currently in a phase of economic, social, and technological transition.

3.1 Environment and Health Concerns

Five months after the June 2012 Rio Summit on green economy and sustainable development, an agreement was reached to extend the Kyoto Protocol. This landmark agreement has two deadlines: (a) 2015 for the development of an extended Kyoto Protocol and, (b) 2020 for its implementation. Unfortunately, global emissions could not be curbed in the run-up to 2012. Emissions picked up again after an initial decline during the economic downturn between 2008 and 2009. Greenhouse

---

This chapter is derived from an article '*Technological and Socioeconomic Issues in the Global Automobile Industry,*' published in Transp. in Dev. Econ. 1: 33, Springer International. doi:10.1007/s40890-015-0005-2. It was later included in the database of US National Academy of Sciences.

A. Bharadwaj, *Environmental Regulations and Innovation in Advanced Automobile Technologies*, SpringerBriefs in Economics,
https://doi.org/10.1007/978-981-10-6952-9_3

gas emissions in 2012 were found to be 20% more than the level in 2000 which, in absolute terms, amount to an additional 50 giga tones of carbon equivalent (UNEP 2012, p. 1). The transport sector already consumes more than 50% of the global oil supply with road transport accounting for 75% of the share. This is despite the fact that transport fuel (at least in most industrialized economies) is taxed more than the fuel for electricity or heating.

Increases in vehicle emissions, particularly in the big cities where cars have emerged as the main contributor towards air pollution, are evident. The problem is exacerbated in the developing countries because of the inefficient public transportation system, lax emission norms, and slow penetration of clean automotive technologies. Beijing's air quality has been reported as being one of the worst in all megacities globally.

According to the Global Burden of Disease Study (2010), outdoor air pollution was responsible for 1.2 million premature deaths in China in 2010, which is approximately 40% of the total number of premature deaths in the world. The study also found that the ambient particulate matter (PM) in emission from vehicles was the fourth leading risk factor for deaths in China. Air pollution ranked seventh on the list of global risk factors according to the same study. The resulting alarm bells renewed efforts to deploy stricter environmental standards, to focus on cleaner transport technologies, and to revitalize efforts to kick-start the electric car industry in China.

Use of biofuels is another contentious area. This is because of a lack of clarity on the exact amount of ethanol (derived from corn), which needs to be blended with gasoline (also called petrol) to increase the octane rating of the fuel. Maize farmers in the USA have been pushing hard to get the amount of ethanol (to be diluted in gasoline) to increase. Power train developers and fuel distillers claim that this will likely damage car engines. Manufacturers, therefore, continue to focus and invest in enhancing the efficiency of the conventional automotive technology of the internal combustion (IC) engine. In terms of performance, innovations in *turbocharging* and *direct fuel injection*, for instance, have made gasoline-powered engines a tough competitor for the hybrid and electric variants. The ushering green movement and environment legislations are certainly driving the car industry to become more environmentally responsible.

3.2 Environmental Regulations and Growth

The relationship between economic growth and environmental quality is vital and multifaceted. International trade through various channels also affects the outcome of this relationship. One side of the classic free trade argument—propelled by the environmentalists—is that unfettered access to world markets and free trade adversely affects the environment because international trade increases the *scale* of economic activity which is per se harmful to the environment and thus trade too is bad for the environment. The other side of the argument—put forth by the proponents of free trade—is that trade stimulates real income but also creates potentially offsetting effects. These effects are the responses to rising incomes in the form of greater demand for better environmental quality and subsequent tightening of environmental policy. This, in turn, is likely to lower "dirty" production techniques and consequently remove harmful effects on the environment.

The trade–environment literature covers the contentious debate on cross-country differences in environmental regulations and their effect on "low regulation" developing countries. According to this *pollution haven effect*, "(…) a tightening up of pollution regulation will, at the margin, have an effect on plant location decisions and trade flows and this phenomenon has a strong theoretical support" (Copeland and Taylor 2004, p. 9).[1] This is different from the so-called *pollution haven hypothesis,* which is the curbing of exports or inflows of capital due to stringent environmental regulation. The argument underlying this hypothesis is that a reduction in trade barriers will lead to migration of polluting industries from countries with stringent regulations to countries with weaker regulations. According to Copeland and Taylor (2004), theoretical support for this hypothesis, in contrast, is quite weak. "Trade theory suggests that many other factors, in addition to pollution regulation, affect trade flows and if these other factors are sufficiently strong, then it is quite possible for there to exist a pollution haven effect, but have the pollution haven hypothesis fail" (Copeland and Taylor 2004, p. 9). In other words, pollution haven effect is necessary, but not sufficient, for the pollution haven hypothesis to hold.

Testing the pollution haven hypothesis for foreign investors in China, Dean et al. (2009) found evidence of pollution haven behavior, but not by investors from developed countries and only in industries that are highly polluting. According to Jaffe et al. (1995, p. 143), the evidence[2] pertaining to the lower levels of net exports in US industries that were subject to relatively stringent environmental regulations was weak[3]. Jorgenson and Wilcoxen (1990) found that environmental regulation decreased US economic growth between 1973 and 1985 by 0.2% per year.

3.3 Environmental Regulation and Innovation

Lyon (1995) found an inverse relationship between regulation ("regulatory hindsight review") and innovation by electric utilities in the USA. He used a theoretical model of electric utility investment behavior where the firm chooses between a

[1]Polluting firms in developed countries may also move to countries for other reasons.

[2]Grossman and Krueger (1993), Kalt (1988), Tobey (1990) all use US trade data and do not find significant effects.

[3]However, recent work suggests that this conclusion was rather weak. According to Copeland and Taylor (2004), most pre-1997 empirical studies testing the link between regulatory stringency and trade investment flows had drawbacks. This was because they (a) used cross-sectional data, (b) were unable to control for unobserved heterogeneity across countries and (c) treated environmental regulations as exogenous.

conventional technology and an innovative technology. He found that a ceiling on earnings due to regulatory intervention discourages firms from adopting risky new technologies, but an earnings floor produces the opposite effect. The study concludes that profit-sharing schemes, properly designed, can promote efficient levels of investment in innovative technologies.

To analyze innovation and diffusion in environmentally responsive technologies, Lanjouw and Mody (1996) used patent data from 1972 to 1986 for USA, Japan, and Germany. They concluded that "the increasing interest in environmental protection over the 1970s and 1980s led to the development of new pollution control technologies" (p. 569). They captured strictness of regulations using (lagged) pollution abatement expenditure in the three countries. Although their analysis is limited to a simple description of central tendencies and variance, they do show a strong correlation between the expenditure and patent variables. Investigating direct policy-induced innovation link,[4] Jaffe and Palmer (1997) used pollution abatement cost for US manufacturing industries as a proxy for stringency of environmental policy and found a positive and statistically significant relationship with R&D expenditure. However, they did not find a statistically significant relationship between regulation and innovation. In the latter regression, their dependent variable was the count of *all* successful patent applications (environmental and non-environmental) as an output measure of innovation activity.

Bhatnagar and Cohen (1997) examined whether more stringent regulation, as measured by higher pollution abatement costs *and* stricter monitoring and enforcement activities, spurs environmental innovation. They estimate a multivariate regression using a panel data set of 146 US manufacturing industries from 1983 to 1992. They go a step ahead by estimating the effect of environmental innovation (as measured by environmentally related patent applications) on industry-wide profitability. They found that (1) more stringent environmental regulation spurs innovation in environmental protection (as measured by the number of environmentally related patent applications), but (2) there is no evidence that these environmental patents increase industry profits. Similar to Bhatnagar and Cohen (1997), Pickman (1998) re-examined Jaffe and Palmer's results of induced innovation in US manufacturing industry. She focused only on environmental patents and uses pollution abatement and control expenditure (PACE) data as a measure of environmental regulation. She found a statistically significant and positive relationship between regulation and innovation using ordinary least square as well as two-staged least-square estimation approach.

[4]Innovation not only refers to technological innovation but can take various other forms such as design innovation, process innovation, or even innovation in marketing techniques (Porter and vander Linde 1995, p. 98).

3.4 Environmental Regulation, Competitiveness, and Firm Performances

Porter (1991) promulgated the view that environmental regulations, in fact, have a positive impact on firms (and the economy) by making them internationally more competitive. A number of studies cropped up to support this view, and almost, the same number of studies emerged negating Porter's arguments. Gabel and Sinclair-Desgag (1998) held the view that X-efficiency (Leibenstein 1966) may be playing a role in pushing firms toward the production possibility frontier by reducing their internal inefficiencies and failures as a result of an exogenous shock of an environmental regulation.

Previously, Tobey (1990), in one of the first thorough empirical studies on this topic, used the cross-sectional Heckscher–Ohlin–Vanek (HOV) model of international trade to ascertain the impact of strict environmental policy on trade patterns in goods produced by the world's "dirty" (in terms of pollution abatement cost) industries.[5] He found that strict regulations in industrialized countries during 1960s and 1970s did not impact trade patterns of the polluting industries.

Using the same HOV methodology, Ratnayake (1998) did not find a negative impact of environmental regulations on New Zealand's trade competitiveness, while Larson et al. (2002) and Xu (2002) found mixed results of regulatory impact on trade competitiveness. Stewart (1993) investigated the potential conflicts between environmental protection and international trade and competition, and concluded that "a nation's imposition of stringent environmental regulation and liability rules may harm its international competitiveness, even though most empirical studies have not established a strong causal association between the two" (p. 2041).

In a frequently cited paper, Jaffe et al. (1995) reviewed studies linking environmental regulation and competitiveness of manufacturing firms in the USA. Their thorough review of the literature at that time suggested that: (1) differences in the strictness of environmental regulations across countries did not influence the competitiveness of US firms and, as a result, did not necessitate a slowdown in regulatory tightening of manufacturing sector, (2) More importantly, despite costs imposed by regulations, they found no observable impact of domestic environmental regulation being detrimental to (or not stimulating) international competitiveness as measured by import and export performance of these firms. They concluded that "overall, there is relatively little evidence to support the hypothesis that environmental regulations have had a large adverse effect on competitiveness, however that elusive term is defined" (p. 157).

---

[5]Heckscher–Ohlin–Vanek model uses factor intensities and trade flows to understand factor intensities. He used a variation of the HOV model to investigate cross-country effects of individual country resource endowments (such as available land, labor, capital, oil, coal.) on trade in specific (dirty) goods.

Xepapadeas and Zeeuw (1999) have made a distinction between the "downsizing effect" and the "modernization effect" of an environmental regulation (specifically, an emission tax).[6] The latter effect can be linked with the observation of Jaffe et al. (1995) that regulation in the 1970s helped speed up the modernization of the US steel manufacturing industry, partly sided with Porter and van der Linde (1995) in claiming that regulation improves industrial competitiveness because it increases the cost of production and, indirectly, leads to a more productive reorganization of current capital stock. They also show that the marginal decrease in profits is lower and marginal decrease in emissions is higher when both effects are present (with heterogeneous capital among firms) compared to when only the first (downsizing effect) effect is present.[7] They conclude that "the trade-off between environmental conditions and profits of the home industry remains but is less sharp because of downsizing and modernization of the industry" (p. 178).

In 2005, the Network of Heads of European Environmental Protection Agencies prepared a report reviewing the evidence on links between environmental regulation and competitiveness in the context of European growth and employment. This report paints a rather rosy and optimistic picture of the ongoing discussion by enumerating all potential benefits of environmental regulation including reduced costs for industry, market creation for environmental goods and services, reducing business risk, creating jobs, driving innovation, increasing competition and investment confidence, improving health of workforce, and protecting natural resources.

More recently, Babool and Reed (2010) test the effect of strict regulations on export competitiveness of manufacturing sectors in 100 ECD countries between 1987 and 2003. They found that environmental regulations can be an effective tool to minimize or stop the flight from the developed countries of industries (shifting plant location) manufacturing environmentally friendly goods. In the different product-based industries included in their study, they found a positive relationship between regulation and net exports in paper products, wood products, and textile products but a negative relationship in most manufacturing industries. Greenstone and Syverson (2012) use the US manufacturing data from 1972 to 1993 to estimate the effect to fair quality regulation[8]on the total factor productivity of the

[6]The downsizing effect is the reduction of total capital stock (and consequently the size) of the firm, while the modernization effect is the reduction in the average age of the total capital stock (consequently increases productivity) (p. 167).

[7]For an opposing view see Feichtinger et al. (2005) who show that an emission tax can have the exact opposite effect, that is, it may lead to an increase in the average age of the total capital stock and thereby reduce productivity.

[8]The authors use pollutant- and county-specific amendments of the 1970 Clean Air Act which required all states to meet National Ambient Air Quality Standards for certain air pollutants such as carbon monoxide, sulfur dioxide, total suspended particulates, ozone, and lead. Environmental regulations in the non-attainment counties were intended to be stringent, while polluting plants located in attainment areas face a more lax regulatory standard (p. 7, 8).

manufacturing plants. They found a 2.6% decline in total factor productivity due to stricter air quality regulations and a staggering $21 billion annual economic cost from the regulation of manufacturing plants in the period studied.[9]

References

Babool, B., & Reed, M. (2010). The impact of environmental policy on international competitiveness in manufacturing. *Applied Economics, 42,* 2317–2326.

Barrett, S. (1994) Strategic environmental policy and intrenational trade. *Journal of Public Economics, 54* (3), 325–338.

Bhatnagar, S., & Cohen, M. A. (1997). The Impact of Environmental Regulation on Innovation: A Panel Data Study, Vanderbilt University (Tennessee) Working Paper.

Copeland, B. R., & Taylor, M. S. (2004). Trade, Growth, and the Environment, *Journal of Economic Literature*, XLII, 771.

Dean, J., Lovely, M., & Wang, H. (2009). Are Foreign Investors Attracted to Weak Environmental Regulations? Evaluating the Evidence from China, *Journal of Development Economics*, *90*, 1–13.

Feichtinger, G., Hartl, R.F., Kort, P.M., & Veliov, V.M. (2005). Environmental Policy, the Porter Hypothesis and the Composition of Capital: Effects of Learning and Technological Progress, *Journal of Environmental Economics and Management*, *50*(2), 434–446.

Gabel, H. L., & Sinclair-Desgagne, B. (1998). The firm, its routines, and the environment. In H. Folmer & T. Tietenberg (Eds.), *The international yearbook of environmental and resource economics 1998/1999: A survey of current issues*. Cheltenham, UK: Edward Elgar.

Greenstone, M., & Syverson, C. (2012). The effects of environmental regulation on the competitiveness of U.S. manufacturing. Department of Economics working paper, University of Chicago.

Grossman, G. M., & Krueger, A. B. (1993). Environmental Impacts of a North American Free Trade Agreement, in Peter M. Garber, ed., The U.S.Mexico free trade agreement. Cambridge, MA: MIT Press, pp. 1356.

Jaffe, A.B., & Palmer, K. (1997). Environmental Regulation and Innovation: A Panel Data Study. *Review of Economics and Statistics*, *79*(4), 610–6.

Jaffe, A. B., Peterson, S. R., Portney, P. R., & Stavins, R. N. (1995). Environmental regulation and the competitiveness of U.S. Manufacturing: What does the evidence tell us? *Journal of Economic Literature, 33*(1), 132–163.

Jorgenson, D. W., & Wilcoxen, P. J. (1990). Environmental Regulation and U.S. Economic Growth *The Rand Journal of Economics*, *21*(2), 314–340.

Kalt, J. (1988). The political economy of protectionism: Tariffs and retaliation in the timber industry, in R. Baldwin, ed., Trade policy issues and empirical analysis. Chicago: University of Chicago Press, pp. 339–364.

Lanjouw, J.O., & Mody, A. (1996). Innovation and the international diffusion of environmentally responsive technology, *Research Policy*, 25(4), 549–571.

Larson, B., Nicolaide, E., Zu'b, B.A., Sukka, N., Larak, K., Matouss, M.S., Zaim, K., & Chouchani, C. (2002). The Impact of Environmental Regulations on Exports: Case Study Results from Cyprus, Jordan, Morocco, Syria, Tunisia, and Turkey, *World Development*, *30*(6), 1057–1072.

[9]They found negative effects in regulations governing ozone, particulates, and sulfur dioxide, while carbon monoxide regulations were found to be positively associated with productivity.

Leibenstein, H. (1966). Allocative efficiency vs. X-efficiency. *American Economic Review, 56,* 392–415.

Lyon, T.P. (1995). Regulatory hindsight review and innovation by electric utilities. *Journal of Regulatory Economics*, *7*(3), 233–254.

Pickman, H. (1998). The effect of environmental regulation on environmental innovation. *Business Strategy and the Environment*, *7* (4), 223–233.

Porter, M. E. (1991). Americas green strategy. *Scientific American, 264*(4), 168.

Porter, M. E., & van der Linde, C. (1995). Toward a new conception of the environment competitiveness relationship. *Journal of Economic Perspectives, 9*(4), 97–118.

Ratnayake, R. (1998). Do stringent environmental regulations reduce international competitiveness? Evidence from an inter-industry analysis. *International Journal of Economics of Business, 5*(1), 77–96.

Rauscher, M. (1994). On Ecological Dumping. Oxford Economic Papers, 46, 822–840.

Stewart, Richard B. (1993). Environmental regulation and international competitiveness. *Yale Law Journal, 102*(8), 2039–2106.

Tobey, J. A. (1990). The effects of domestic environmental policies on patterns of world trade: An empirical test. *Kyklos, 2,* 191–209.

UNEP. (2012). The Emissions Gap Report 2012, United Nations Environment Programme, Nairobi.

Ulph, A. (1996). Environmental Policy and International Trade when Governments and Producers Act Strategically. *Journal of Environmental Economics and Management*, *30*(3), 265–281.

Xu, X. (2002). International Trade and Environmental Regulation: Time Series Evidence and Cross Section Test. *Environmental and Resource Economics*, *17*, 233–257.

Xepapadeas, A. & Zeeuw, D. A. (1999). Environmental Policy and Competitiveness: The Porter Hypothesis and the Composition of Capital. *Journal of Environmental Economics and Management*, *37*, 165–182.

Chapter 4
Role of State and Regulatory Instruments

Abstract The aim of this chapter is to obtain present information about the environmental legislations and the overall development of standards and norms relevant to the transport industry in Germany, India, China, and Brazil. It is evident that Germany, as part of a bigger commitment by Europe, led the way in setting performance targets, imposing binding emission limits, and helping the industry adjust to all these changes. The other countries followed this path making necessary technical changes to the regulations to suit local needs. The implementation and adoption of new measures were done at different times in these countries. Even though India has had a structured vehicular pollution control plan since early 1990s, it was very slow in keeping pace with the changing environment and industrial development. China, on the other hand, joined the regulatory bandwagon very late but it took the right decisions within the last decade to catch up with others. The Brazilian case was slightly different from its counterparts. Brazil, like India, started early and, like China, decided to push its reform agenda in the right direction in the 1990s and early 2000s. However, Brazil failed to keep the momentum going because of which it now lags behind other countries in adopting stricter regulations.

4.1 Environmental Regulation—Design and Instruments

A generic definition of regulation is the implementation of rules by public authorities and governmental bodies to influence market activity and the behavior of private actors in the economy. An intervention by a government with the objective of protecting the environment in any form by influencing, directly or indirectly, human activities and actions can broadly be referred to as environmental regulation. The primary objective of an environmental regulation is to protect the environment and health of all life forms from anthropogenic environmental damage. The damage occurs due to exposure to hazardous substances and pollutants released by products and processes developed by firms. There are three broad classes of regulatory instruments[1]:

[1]Classification by OECD (1997) and Nelissen and Requate (2004).

A. Bharadwaj, *Environmental Regulations and Innovation in Advanced Automobile Technologies*, SpringerBriefs in Economics,
https://doi.org/10.1007/978-981-10-6952-9_4

1. Command-and-control policies
2. Market-based economic instruments
3. Voluntary agreements.

Command-and-control instruments such as emission standards and technological limits, along with administrative obligations and prohibitions, are the most common forms of environmental regulation. They are collectively referred as "legal instruments." These instruments directly impact the activity that affects the environment and force the polluter to adopt the "best available technology." Market-based instruments, on the other hand, are economic instruments that are intended to give incentives or disincentives to reduce emissions through pollution taxes, permits, and subsidies on emission abatement. Voluntary agreements are institutional arrangements (both private and public), which are devised to improve the environmental performance of firms through credible commitments and information disclosure.

In the classic 1971 work, Baumol and Oats discussed the merits of economic instruments that give incentives to firms to attain the benchmark standard of optimal environmental quality—referred as the "ambient standard." The legal perspective of environmental standards is contrasting. It refers to regulatory measures imposed by government agencies on the actual source of the negative environmental externality. Despite the dichotomy, both legal and economic regulatory instruments are classified as *ex-ante* regulation.

Cropper and Oates (1992, p. 685) explained that the determination of environmental policy is a two-step process. *First*, standards or targets for environmental quality are set, and, *second*, a regulatory system is designed and put in place to achieve these standards. They describe that "Under the Clean Air Act, the first task of the US Environmental Protection Agency (EPA) was to set standards in the form of maximum permissible concentration of the major air pollutants. The next step was to design a regulatory plan to attain these standards for air quality."

Ex-post regulation, on the other hand, tackles problems of identification of the polluter, costs involved in the cleanup, and restoration of the damages caused by the actions of the polluter. Regulations can, *ex-ante*, provide incentives for the involved parties to take precautions to avoid environmental harm and to minimize risk of environmental damage. *Ex-post*, the regulation can enable recovery of costs associated with the resulting damage and help compensate the victim(s), as the case may be.[2] In reality, the two regulatory systems may be complementary (Kolstad et al. 1990; Schmitz 2000). Ultimately, the choice of regulatory instrument is a complex decision which is dependent on the source of pollution and the precise nature of resulting environmental damage.

[2]See Shavell (1984) for a comparison of the two regulatory systems based on four broad determinants—difference in knowledge about risky activities possessed by private parties and by a regulatory authority, capacity to pay for the full magnitude of harm done, threat of suit for harm done, and various administrative costs incurred by private parties and by the public in connection with the use of the legal system and with regulation.

Environmental regulations relevant for the transport sector encompass multiple laws concerning protection of environment and human health but they often take the form of emission standards that prescribe a threshold limit for pollutants. Emission standards, as regulatory measures, take the center stage because through them, both quality and quantity of all major pollutants are regulated.

4.2 Environmental Regulations in the Automotive Industry

The automotive industry is evolving rapidly on multiple dimensions such as technological innovation, adoption of stricter government regulations, and structural shifts with changing consumer preferences. Several countries have put in place policies to address transport issues including emission norms and fuel efficiency standards. According to An and Sauer (2004), fuel economy programs and emission targets (mandatory or voluntary) are one of the most cost-effective instruments to tackle oil demand and vehicular emissions.

Jaffe et al. (2005) suggest that the market failures (associated with environmental pollution, innovation, and diffusion of new technologies) provide a strong rationale for environmental policies that foster emission reduction as well as the development and adoption of environmentally beneficial technology. According to them, weak or non-existent environmental policies lead to lower than socially optimum investments in development and diffusion of environment-friendly technologies.

Economic expansion and increased mobility has, among other reasons, increased fuel consumption in all countries. Nevertheless, USA, Japan, and Europe are leaders in implementing strict but effective environmental regulations. They have shown the way for other countries, which end up adopting the regulatory and technological path taken by Europe or USA. The last decade witnessed a range of regulations proposed and adopted in these countries, many of which resulted in impressive decline in emission levels and increase in fuel economy standards. India, China, and Brazil entered the international emission regulation stage much later but since then the gap has been converging rapidly.

Figure 4.1 shows the air pollution levels in some of the megacities, which are also some of the most densely populated regions of the world. The level of particulate matter (PM10, a toxic pollutant emitted mainly by vehicles) differs widely across cities in developed countries relative to those in the developing countries.

Different types of environment policy instruments can be used for the purpose of reducing the environmental impact of vehicles. A summary of these instruments is presented in Table 4.1. This study focuses on technological innovations that are part of Stage 1 through Stage 3.

The rest of the chapter traces the origins and evolution of environmental legislations and regulatory changes relevant to the transport industry in Germany, India, China, and Brazil. It should be noted that only regulations which are

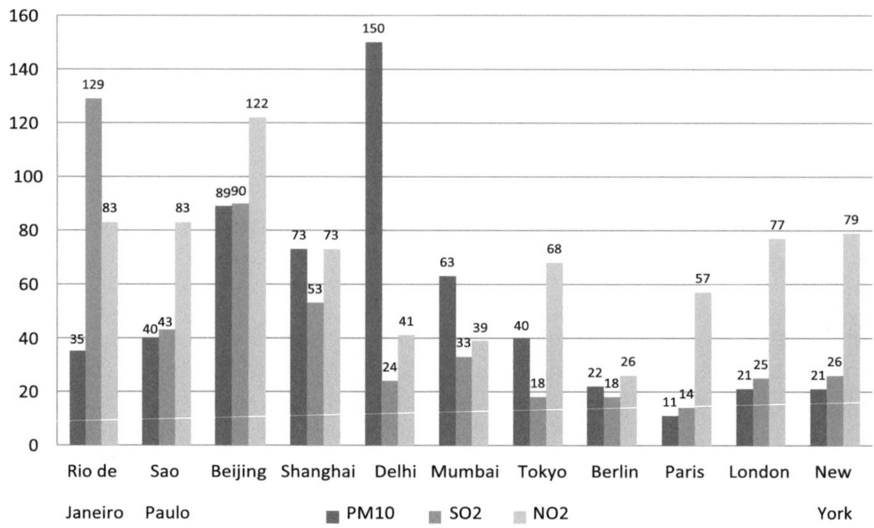

Fig. 4.1 Emission levels in selected cities: developing versus developed cities. *Note* PM10 (2004), SO_2 (1998–01), NO_2 (1995–01). *Source* Pandey et al. (2006)

Table 4.1 Policy instruments to curb environmental impact of vehicles

Stage	Impact point	Target group	Govt. intervention
Stage 0	Vehicle use	Consumers and producers	Labeling of fuel standards, better public transport, scrapping old vehicles
Stage 1: Precombustion	Fuel content and quality	Fuel producers, gas-station owners	Differential taxation (tax incentive for cleaner alternatives), fuel composition, phasing-out specific fuel content (ex. lead and sulfur content)
Stage 2: Combustion	Engine modifications	Vehicle component manufacturer	Emission standards, mandatory use of less polluting modes (ex. CNG)
Stage 3: Postcombustion	Exhaust treatment	Vehicle component manufacturer	Technological standards (ex. catalytic converter)
Stage 4	Behavioral changes	Consumers and producers	Pollution certification (PUC), emission fee, tradable permits, parking changes

Adapted from Kathuria (2002)

associated with pollutants in vehicular emissions, fuel content, fuel consumption, and technology standards applicable to passenger cars as well as medium and heavy commercial vehicles.

4.2.1 Germany

Vehicular emissions in the European Union have originally been regulated by *Directive 70/220/EEC* for light-duty vehicles (passenger cars and light vans) and by *Directive 88/77/EC* for heavy-duty vehicles (trucks and buses), and the amendments therein. The statutory regulations controlling emissions and several successive amendments have become gradually more stringent. The list below traces the history of the changing landscape of the European environmental legislation for the transport sector.

- *Council Directive 70/220/EEC adopted on March 20, 1970*: The first directive to deal with approximation of the laws of the Member States relating to measures to be taken against air pollution by gases from positive-ignition engines of motor vehicles. Directive 70/220/EEC remained the basis for all EU wide regulations on vehicular emissions from passenger cars and light commercial vehicles until 2007. Regulation 715/2007 replaced previous standards and was now directly enforceable in all Member States.
- *Council Directive 88/77/EEC* regulated emissions from heavy-duty diesel trucks and buses and was also amended multiple times. European Regulation 595/2009 governs the current limits. Even though pollutants emitted by light vehicles are almost the same as those emitted by heavy vehicles, the difference in testing procedures and vehicle size is the reason why they are covered by separate directives.
- Regulations for both categories of vehicles were aligned in 1992 through a series of standards, which are known as the Euro norms. Emission regulations of passenger cars and other light vehicles are referred as Euro 1, 2, 3, 4, 5, and 6, and for heavy-duty vehicles as Euro I, II, III, IV, V, and VI, respectively. For gasoline passenger car, restrictions are placed on emission of carbon monoxide (CO), hydrocarbons (HC), and nitrous oxide (NO_x). The original *Directive 70/220/EEC* sets limits for CO and HC, while the limits on NO_x were introduced in a 1977 amendment. Since this *Commission Directive 77/102/EEC,* all three pollutants were reduced in tandem.

It should be noted that for cars that run on gasoline, the procedure for testing emissions is based on six test cycles under differing conditions. Table 4.2 depicts the tightening of limits for all emission norms for gasoline-run passenger cars.

- The regulations that guided gasoline cars initially covered diesel-fueled passenger cars as well. However, after the adoption of regulations pertaining to particulate matter (PM) in 1988 under the *Council Directive 88/436/EEC*, the separation between regulations on vehicles run by the two fuels was introduced. The test procedure for diesel-run cars is also different. Table 4.3 depicts the tightening of limits for all emission norms for diesel-run passenger cars.
- *Directive 70/220/EEC* was implemented in early 1970s and governed all pre-Euro regulations. This was the main amendment in the legislation that led to the creation of successive Euro norms. *Directive 91/441/EEC* (also known as

Table 4.2 EU emission norms for gasoline-run passenger cars

Standard		Approval date	CO	HC	HC + NO_x	NO_x	PM
Euro	1	01.07.1992	2.72		0.97		
Euro	2	01.01.1996	2.20		0.50		
Euro	3	01.01.2000	2.30	0.20	0.50	0.15	
Euro	4	01.01.2005	1.0	0.10		0.08	
Euro	5	01.09.2009	1.0	0.10		0.06	0.005[a]
Euro	6	01.09.2014	1.0	0.10		0.06	0.005[a]

CO carbon monoxide, *HC* hydrocarbons, *NO_x* nitrous oxide, *PM* particulate matter. Prescribed limits for all pollutants in grams per kilometer
[a]Applicable to direct injection engines only

Table 4.3 EU emission norms for diesel-run passenger cars

Standard		Approval date	CO	HC + NO_x	NO_x	PM
Euro	1	01.07.1992	2.72	0.97		0.14
Euro	2	01.01.1996	1.0	0.70		0.08
Euro	3	01.01.2000	0.64	0.56	0.50	0.05
Euro	4	01.01.2005	0.50	0.30	0.25	0.025
Euro	5a	01.09.2009	0.50	0.23	0.18	0.005
Euro	5b[a]	01.09.2011	0.50	0.23	0.18	0.005
Euro	6	01.09.2014	0.50	0.17	0.08	0.005

CO carbon monoxide, *HC* hydrocarbons, *NO_x* nitrous oxide, *PM* particulate matter. Prescribed limits for all pollutants in grams per kilometer
[a]Introduced additional requirement on the count of PM per kilometer

EC93) was the launch pad for Euro 1 norm, which was implemented in July 1992 exclusively for passenger cars.

- *Directive 94/12/EC, Directive 96/69/EC, and Directive 96/44/EC* led to the creation of Euro 2 norm in January 1996. The first two were amendments to the Directive 70/220/EC, while the third is referred to as EC96. These regulations saw the first adoption of a PM limit and mandated fitting of compliant engines immediately after production.
- *Directive 98/69/EC* (and amendments 98/77/EC, 1999/102/EC, 2001/1/EC, 2001/100/EC, 2000/80/EC, and 2002/80/EC) comprises the regulations that led to the implementation of Euro 3 norm in January 2000. Also known as EC2000, this third phase of emission legislation sets limits on nitrogen oxide (NO_x) in addition to HC + NO_x. Cars, for the first time, underwent a new transient test cycle very similar to actual on-road driving, rather than simulations conducted in controlled environments.
- *Regulations 715/2007 and 692/2008* finally implemented the Euro 5. For diesel engines, this was introduced in two different stages but for gasoline engines the only governing norm was Euro 5. In September 2009, Euro 5 and Euro 5a were introduced, while Euro 5b, introduced in September 2011, for the first time

included a particle number emission limit for compression ignition engines. In September 2014, EU launched the Euro 6 emission norm. Along with improved versions of SCR and EGR systems, diesel particulate filter (DPF) technology are now fully embraced by the manufacturers. The Euro 6 also mandate fulfillment of the Enhanced Environmentally Friendly Vehicle (EEV) emission levels for complex IC engines, electric hybrid diesel and natural gas engines that require additional particulate filtration.

The modalities of the implementation of carbon dioxide emissions from passenger vehicles for year 2020 under the *European Regulation 443/2009/EC* are underway. Relative to the 2015 baseline 130 g CO_2/km, an emission target of 95 g CO_2/km for 2020 for new passenger vehicles is expected to ameliorate air quality, lower import bills, and reduce oil dependence. Apart from these macroeconomic benefits, this target is expected to reduce fuel costs and increase fuel savings for the consumers.

4.2.2 India

In January 1985, the Department of Environment (which is now the Ministry of Environment and Forests, MoEF), Automotive Research Association of India (ARAI), and the Central Pollution Control Board (CPCB) constituted an expert committee to finalize (1) India's first emission standards for road transport and manufacturing, (2) vehicle testing methods, and (3) establishment of specialized labs to carry out these tests. The recommendations of the committee to implement mass and in-use vehicular emission norms and appropriate testing methods were later notified under the Environment Protection Act 1986.[3]

- Since then, automotive regulations in India are governed by the nodal Ministry of Shipping, Road Transport and Highways. *The Motor Vehicles Act, 1988 (MVA),* and the *Central Motor Vehicles Rules, 1989 (CMVR),* govern the emission norms and safety standards pertaining to motor vehicles in India.
- The first instance of regulation was the idling carbon monoxide and free acceleration smoke regulations introduced in the State of Maharashtra in 1984. The idle emission norms became effective throughout the nation in 1989. In February 1990, the first mass and in-use emission norms were prescribed in India due to the Second Amendment Rule 1990 under *Section 25, Environment (Protection) Act 1986*. The Sakia Committee was constituted by the Supreme Court of India to assess the available emission control technologies in the world and in India and to examine the feasibility of operating vehicles on Indian roads that comply with the new regulations.

[3]The following historical time line was adapted from CPCB (2010) and MoEF (2010).

- The idle emission standards were officially replaced by mass emission norms for petrol in 1991 and for diesel in 1992. The exhaust emission norms for petrol-run vehicles below 3.5 ton gross vehicle weight (GVW) covered only carbon monoxide and hydrocarbon pollutants, while the diesel-run vehicle regulations covered full load and free acceleration smoke emission. The recommendations in the Sakia Committee Report 1991 included phasing-out leaded petrol, introducing unleaded petrol (with New Delhi as the pilot) by April 1992, prescribing standards for different vehicular pollutants, strengthening enforcement-monitoring mechanisms, financing local R&D in advanced emission control technologies, making it compulsory for all petrol-run vehicles to retrofit catalytic converters to control CO and HC emissions and suitable devices for diesel-run vehicles to control particulate matter and smoke with effect from April 1992, initiating pipeline network for compressed natural gas supply for use as vehicle fuel.
- In 1992, the exhaust mass emission norms for diesel engines were extended to vehicles above 3.5 ton GVW. In the same year, MoEF drafted (1) the *National Conservation Strategy and Policy Statement on Environment and Development*, and (2) *Policy Statement for Abatement of Pollution*, which identified National Ambient Air Quality Standards (NAAQS) for different pollutants. In May 1991, Mathur Committee started discussing mass emission norms for vehicles for year 1995 and 2000.
- In 1992, CPCB recommended providing cleaner diesel and petrol for vehicles by 1995. In October 1994, the Supreme Court of India passed an order directing the agencies to (1) supply petrol with TEL less than 0.15 g per L to entire country by December 1996 and (2) to supply completely unleaded petrol in all major cities by April 1995.

A result of these deliberations was implementation of the following regulations:

- (1) From April 1995, petrol with lead content of less than 0.013 g per L was supplied in all metropolitan cities. (2) All new vehicles on sale in the metropolitan cities from April 1995 will have catalytic converters installed. (3) Sulfur content in diesel supplied in these cities was brought down to 0.5%.
- In April 1996, stringent norms were laid for gasoline and diesel engines for carbon monoxide and combined emission limit for hydrocarbon and nitrogen oxide. Further, evaporative emissions were stipulated to be below 2 g per test for petrol engines. In August 1997, under the Motor Vehicle Act, emission norms equivalent to the Euro I norms were notified to take effect from April 2000. In the same year, the entire fleet of public transport in New Delhi was converted to CNG. In the following year, the Pollution Control Authority issued notice to phase out all diesel-run public transport vehicles and strict adherence of all private vehicles to Euro II equivalent emission norms.

- In 1999, India Stage I emission norms were notified in the entire country in year 2000 and were renamed Bharat Stage I covering all categories of vehicles. These were replaced in four metro cities by the Euro II equivalent norms in 2001 called Bharat Stage II emissions norms, wherein particulate limit values were introduced for diesel-run vehicles. These norms were introduced for passenger vehicles up to GVW of 3.5 tons from April 2000 and for heavy vehicles from October 2001.
- Bharat Stage III (equivalent to Euro III) norms for petrol- and diesel-run vehicles were adopted in 11 metro cities in April 2005. At the same time, the previous BS-II norms were extended to cover the entire country. Table 4.4 depicts the emission limits for petrol-run vehicles.
- From 1995, all manufacturers were mandated to install catalytic converters in all passenger vehicles. Moreover, all petrol-run vehicles manufactured from April 1996 were fitted with (1) positive crankcase ventilation systems, while the in-use pre-1996 models were retrofitted with these systems in order to reduce total hydrocarbon emissions and (2) evaporative emission control systems to absorb fuel vapors from fuel tanks and carburetor fuel bowl.
- From April 1998, the testing method was changed from hot start to cold start for all passenger vehicles. Euro I equivalent norms, implemented in 2000, required modifications in engine design, mainly in fuel injection for improved fuel economy (Table 4.5).

The Central Pollution Control Board published the National Ambient Air Quality Standards in November 2009 in the official Gazette of India under Section 16 (Subsection 2 h) of the Air (Prevention and Control of Pollution) Act

Table 4.4 India emission norms for petrol-run vehicles

Standard	Year	CO	HC	NO_x	HC + NO_x
Mass emission norms	1991	14.3–27.1	2.0–2.9		
Mass emission norms	1996	8.68–12.4			3.0–4.36
Mass emission norms	1998	4.34–6.20			1.5–2.18
India Stage I	1999	2.72			0.97
Bharat Stage IIa[a]	2000	2.2			0.5
Bharat Stage IIb[b]	2003	2.2–5.0			0.5–0.7
Bharat Stage III	2005	2.30	0.20	0.15	
Bharat Stage IV	2010	1.0	0.10	0.08	

CO Carbon monoxide, *HC* hydrocarbons, NO_x nitrous oxide. Prescribed limits for all pollutants in grams per kilometer with a deterioration factor of 1.2

[a]Norms tightened using a modified Indian Driving Cycle (IDC) method, applicable for up to six-seater passenger vehicles with a gross vehicle weight up to 2500 kg

[b]For more than six-seater vehicles with a gross vehicle weight up to 2500 kg

Table 4.5 India emission norms for diesel-run vehicles

Standard	Year	CO	HC	NO_x	HC + NO_x	PM
GVW 3.5 tons: by engine dynamometer in g/kWh						
Mass norms	1992	14.0	3.5	18.0		
Mass norms	1996	11.20	2.40	14.40		
Mass norms	2000	4.5	1.1	8.0		0.36–0.61[a]
Bharat Stage II	2003	4.0	1.1	7.0		0.15
Bharat Stage III	2005	2.1	1.6	5.0		0.10
GVW 3.5 tons: by chassis dynamometer in g/km						
Mass norms	1992	17.3–32.6	2.7–3.7			
Mass norms	1996	5.0–9.0			2.0–4.0	
Mass norms	2000	2.7–6.9			0.97–1.7	0.14–0.25
Bharat Stage II	2003	1.0–1.5			0.7–1.2	0.08–0.17
Bharat Stage III	2005	0.64–0.95		0.5–0.78	0.56–0.86	0.05–0.10
GVW > 3.5 tons: by engine dynamometer in g/kwh						
Mass norms	1992	17.3–32.6	2.7–3.7			
Mass norms	1996	11.20	2.40	14.40		
Mass norms	2000	4.5	1.1	8.0		0.36[a]
Bharat Stage II	2003	4.0	1.1	7.0		0.15
Bharat Stage III[b]	2005	2.1	0.66	5.0		0.10–0.13
Bharat Stage IV[c]	2010	1.5	0.46	3.5		0.02
Passenger cars: by chassis dynamometer in g/km						
Bharat Stage II[d]	2003	1.0			0.7	0.8
Bharat Stage II[e]	2003	1.0–1.5			0.7–1.2	0.08–0.17
Bharat Stage III[d]	2005	0.64		0.50	0.56	0.05
Bharat Stage III[e]	2005	0.64–0.95		0.5–0.78	0.56–0.86	0.05–0.10
Bharat Stage IV[d]	2010	0.05		0.25	0.30	0.025
Bharat Stage IV[e]	2010	0.05–0.74		0.25–0.39	0.30–0.46	0.025–0.06

GVW gross vehicle weight, *CO* carbon monoxide, *HC* hydrocarbons, NO_x nitrous oxide

[a]For engines with power exceeding 85 kW

[b]Prescribed limit for smoke = $0.8\ m^{-1}$

[c]Prescribed limit for smoke = $0.5\ m^{-1}$

[d]For up to six-seater vehicles with a gross vehicle weight up to 2500 kg

[e]For more than six-seaters with a gross vehicle weight up to 3500 kg

1981 and in supersession of the notification numbers S.O. 384(E) of April 1994 and S.O. 935(E) of October 1998. Table 4.6 illustrates the standards by pollutants.

There has been a huge delay in announcing and adopting corporate average fuel economy standards for 2015 and 2020 in India, which can seriously impact energy security and environmental plans. By comparison, as Table 4.7 shows, USA, EU, and even China have made substantial improvements in adopting effective and efficient fuel economy standards.

Table 4.6 Indian National Ambient Air Quality Standards 2009

Pollutant		General areas[a]	Sensitive areas[b]
Sulfur dioxide	(SO_2)	50	20
Nitrogen dioxide	(NO_2)	40	30
Particulate matter	(PM_{10})	60	60
Particulate matter	($PM_{2.5}$)	40	40
Ozone	(O_2)	100	100
Lead	(Pb)	0.50	0.50
Carbon monoxide	(CO)	0.20	0.20
Ammonia	(NH_3)	100	100
Benzene	(C_6H_6)	0.5	0.5
Arsenic	(As)	0.6	0.6
Nikel	(Ni)	20	20

[a]Annual arithmetic mean of minimum 104 measurements per year at a particular site taken twice a week 24 hourly at uniform intervals

[b]All pollutants measured in μ g/m^3 except arsenic and nickel, which are measured in n g/m^3 concentration in ambient air in industrial, residential, rural, and other areas

[c]Concentration in ambient air in ecologically sensitive areas as notified by the Central Government

Table 4.7 Comparison of Corporate Average Fuel Economy Standards (2010 & 2020)

Region	2010	2020
USA	187	121
Europe	145	95
Japan	130	105
China	179	117
India	141	122[a]

Emission measured in CO_2 g/km

[a]Original proposal

4.2.3 China

Environmental regulations on vehicular emissions in China are guided by three legislations, namely:

1. Environmental Protection Law of the People's Republic of China, 1979
2. Law of the People's Republic of China on the Prevention and Control of Air Pollution, 1987

3. Detailed Rules and Regulations for the Law of the People's Republic of China on the Prevention and Control of Air Pollution, 1991.

Environmental regulations for the transport sector, specifically emission standards, are framed and adopted at the federal level by the State Environmental Protection Administration (SEPA) based on these laws.[4] More recently, the Ministry of Environmental Protection (MEP) and the Standardization Administration of China (SAC) are issuing emission standards jointly, and SEPA has taken the responsibility of drafting and giving the final approval. A brief (and rather recent) history of Chinese legislations in the automobile domain is presented below.[5]

- China enacted the *China Clean Air Law* in 1987, which provided legislative basis for mobile emission control. SEPA drafted regulation *GB-11641-89* for light-duty vehicles in 1989, which was applicable to passenger cars, passenger vans, and light-freight vehicles of *GV W* 3500 kg operating at a minimum speed of 50 km/h.
- *Regulation GB 14761* was the first regulation in PRC targeting automobile emissions and was implemented in the 1990s. Regulatory standards adopted for light-duty vehicles and crankcase emissions for gasoline vehicles in China in July 1990 were roughly equivalent to the European ECE Regulation 1503. In 1993, a new fuel evaporation standard using trap method was eventually adopted.
- In 1995, the Clean Air Law was revised and the State Council was given the primary authority to regulate vehicular emissions. As pilot regulations, Beijing and Shanghai implemented Euro 1 equivalent emission norms and started supply of unleaded gasoline in 1999. In the following year, the act was revised again to give MEP the sole authority to set emission standards at a national level. It was the first time in China that emission limits were set based on ambient air quality as well as economic and technological considerations.
- *China 1 emission norms* for light-duty vehicles were implemented nationwide in January 2000 and were based on Euro 1 norms. In the following year, *China 2 emission norms*, based on Euro 2, were introduced in the pilot cities of Beijing (August 2002) and Shanghai (March 2003) before nationwide implementation in two phases. In Phase 1, the norms were implemented in July 2004 for vehicles with positive-ignition (gasoline and natural gas) engines. In Phase 2, they were implemented in September 2003 for vehicles with compression ignition engines. Tables 4.8 and 4.9 list all subsequent emission standards for gasoline and diesel vehicles implemented in China since 2005.

---

[4]Chinese authorities follow certain naming conventions for their environmental regulations. "GB" refers to mandatory standards at the national level, "GB/T" refers to standards that are recommended by the agencies, and "HJ" are specific environmental standards, while "BJ" and "SH" stand for Beijing and Shanghai, respectively.

[5]The information for this analysis is derived from multiple sources including MEP Environmental Reports as available on the Web site, diesel net group, and Faiz et al. (1996).

Table 4.8 Chinese emission norms for gasoline (positive ignition) vehicles

Standard	Year	Category	(Class)[a]	CO	HC	NMHC	NOx	PM
China 3[b]	2005	Type 1		2.3	0.20		0.15	
	2005	Type 2	(I)	2.3	0.20		0.15	
	2005	Type 2	(II)	4.17	0.25		0.18	
	2005	Type 2	(III)	5.22	0.29		0.21	
China 4	2008	Type 1		1.0	0.10		0.08	
	2008	Type 2	(I)	1.0	0.10		0.08	
	2008	Type 2	(II)	1.81	0.13		0.10	
	2008	Type 2	(III)	2.27	0.16		0.11	
China 5	2013	Type 1		1.0	0.10	0.068	0.06	0.0045[c]
	2013	Type 2	(I)	1.0	0.10	0.068	0.06	0.0045[c]
	2013	Type 2	(II)	1.81	0.13	0.068	0.075	0.0045[c]
	2013	Type 2	(III)	2.27	0.16	0.068	0.82	0.0045[c]

CO carbon monoxide, *HC* hydrocarbons, *NMHC* non-methane hydrocarbons, NO_x nitrous oxide, *PM* particulate matter. Prescribed limits in grams per kilometer

[a]Categorization of light-duty vehicles based on modified EU classification. Type 1 vehicles = M_1 vehicles for up to six passengers and *GVW* 2.5 tons. Type 2 vehicles = other LDVs including N_1 light commercial vehicles divided into three classes based on reference mass (RM). Class I: *RM* 1305 kg, Class II: 1305 kg < *RM* < 1760 kg, Class III: *RM* > 1760 kg

[b]Also includes implementation of European on-board diagnostic (OBD) regulations from 2006

[c]Applies only to direct injection positive-ignition gasoline engines

Table 4.9 Emission norms for diesel (compression ignition) vehicles

Standard	Year	Category	(Class)[a]	CO	HC + NO_x	NO_x	PM
China 3	2005	Type 1		0.64	0.56	0.50	0.05
	2005	Type 2	(I)	0.64	0.56	0.50	0.05
	2005	Type 2	(II)	0.80	0.72	0.65	0.07
	2005	Type 2	(III)	0.95	0.86	0.78	0.10
China 4	2008	Type 1		0.50	0.30	0.25	0.025
	2008	Type 2	(I)	0.50	0.30	0.25	0.025
	2008	Type 2	(II)	0.63	0.39	0.33	0.040
	2008	Type 2	(III)	0.74	0.46	0.39	0.060
China 5[b]	2013	Type 1		0.50	0.230	0.180	0.0045[c]
	2013	Type 2	(I)	0.50	0.230	0.180	0.0045[c]
	2013	Type 2	(II)	0.63	0.295	0.235	0.0045[c]
	2013	Type 2	(III)	0.74	0.350	0.280	0.0045[c]

CO carbon monoxide, *HC* hydrocarbons, *NMHC* non-methane hydrocarbons, NO_x nitrous oxide, *PM* particulate matter. Prescribed limits in grams per kilometer

[a]Categorization of light-duty vehicles based on modified EU classification. Type 1 vehicles = M_1 vehicles for up to six passengers and *GVW* 2.5 tons. Type 2 vehicles = other LDVs including N_1 light commercial vehicles divided into three classes based on reference mass (RM). Class I: *RM* 1305 kg, Class II: 1305 kg < *RM* < 1760 kg, Class III: *RM* > 1760 kg

[b]Similar to Euro 5, China 5 legislation also introduced a *particle number* (*PN*) emission limit of 610^{11} PNs/km

- Emission norms for heavy-duty commercial vehicles were adopted in 1983 under *Regulation GB-3842-83, Regulation GB-3843-83, and Regulation 3844-83*. These regulations collectively prescribed limits for carbon monoxide and hydrocarbons (determined at idle speed) applicable to both new and in-use vehicles.
- For passenger cars, tail pipe mass emissions became effective from January 2000 based on the European Euro 1 norm emanating from *Regulation 91/441/EEC*. In the same year, tail pipe emissions from light trucks were restricted in October 2000 on the basis of Euro 1 norms (*93/59/EEC*).
- China issued limits to control smoke from heavy-duty diesel vehicles (primarily used for freight and commercial transport) in 1985. The implementation of this standard promoted improvement in diesel engine quality (EPB of Chongqing 2002). The actual engine modifications occurred with the implementation of the Euro 1 equivalent standard in the year 2000.
- The amended Law of the People's Republic of China on the Prevention and Control of Air Pollution started phasing out of leaded gasoline in 1995 and was encouraged in the Air Law 2000. The phaseout was planned in two steps in China—started in July 1999 in major Chinese cities, followed by requiring all refineries throughout the country to produce only unleaded gasoline starting January 2000. A nationwide ban on leaded gasoline was brought in July 2000. Introduction of these regulations created conditions to implement stricter standards and adoption of advanced technologies such as electronic fuel injection and three-way catalytic converter.
- In the year 2005, Beijing's Environment Pollution Bureau (EPB) pushed for Euro 3 for gasoline-run vehicles and Euro 4 for diesel-run vehicles in light of the 2008 Olympics held in Beijing. Similarly, Shanghai's EPB pushed for leapfrogging to Euro 4 to make standards stricter and to catch up with regulations in other countries.
- For heavy-duty commercial vehicles, China has been following in the footsteps of Europe. Chinese emission standards for heavy trucks and buses (China III–V) are based on Euro III–V.
- In 2010, new air quality regulations were introduced in China to bring all provinces, autonomous regions, and municipalities directly under the net of the State Council to frame and implement stricter policies to improve quality of air (Table 4.10).

According to UNESCAP (2011), the regulations include four strategies that specifically address the reduction of vehicular emissions: (1) strict implementation of national vehicular emission standards, (2) improve the vehicular environmental management system, (3) accelerate the use of clean vehicle fuels, and (4) development of public transportation.

Table 4.10 Overview of trends by emissions standards in 2009

Standard	Adhering vehicles in million (% total)	CO	HC	NOx	PM
		2009 emissions in MMT (% of total)			
Pre-China I	10.6 (17.1%)	15.55 (50.0%)	1.92 (53.5%)	2.61 (49.6%)	0.31 (55.9%)
China I	15.9 (25.7%)	10.26 (33.0%)	1.05 (29.5%)	1.52 (29.5%)	0.15 (28.4%)
China II	19.7 (31.8%)	4.15 (13.4%)	0.43 (12.2%)	0.79 (14.9%)	0.07 (12.8%)
China III	15.7 (25.4%)	1.12 (3.6%)	0.17 (4.8%)	0.31 (6.0%)	0.01 (2.9%)

CO carbon monoxide, *HC* hydrocarbons, NO_x nitrous oxide, *PM* particulate matter. Emissions in year 2009 measured in million metric tons
Adapted from the China Vehicle Emission Control Annual Report 2010, MEP

4.2.4 Brazil

There are two nodal agencies under the Brazilian Ministry of Environment (Ministériodo Meio Ambiente) that are responsible for the development and implementation of standards for vehicular emissions, namely:

1. Brazilian Institute of Environment and Renewable Natural Resources, IBAMA (*Instituto Brasileirodo Meio Ambiente e dos Recursos Naturais Renovaveis*)
2. National Council for the Environment, CONAMA (*Conselho Nacional do Meio Ambiente*).

These agencies regulate vehicular emissions within the two CONAMA programs listed below. The focus of this study is only on the first regulatory program designed for motor vehicles. Brazilian regulations for light- and heavy-duty vehicles, under this program, are based on both US and EU regulations.[6]

1. *PROCONVE*—Air Pollution Control Program for Motor Vehicles (*Programa de Controlled Poluiçãodo Arpor Veículos Automotores*)
2. *PROMOT*—Air Pollution Control Program for Motorcycles and Similar Vehicles (*Programa de Controleda Poluiçãodo Arpor Motociclose Veículos Similares*).

- Most relevant regulatory and legislative steps taken in the recent past are highlighted below.[7] Emission standards for light motor vehicles are

[6]Like India, Brazilian regulators tailor these adopted regulations to suit their own local needs. It could be in the form of slightly different prescribed limits or different testing methods and techniques.

[7]Information for this historical background is adapted from the Environmental Collection, Guidelines–Environmental Management No. 3, Ministry of Environment, Brasilia (IBAMA, 2011), and transport policy (dot) net, a joint effort by the International Council for Clean Transportation (ICCT) and Diesel Net.

categorized in two groups—light passenger vehicles (automobiles) and light commercial vehicles. PROCONVE L standards apply to vehicles of GVW up to 3856 kg and curb weight up to 2720 kg.[8]

- Emission limits prescribed under *PROCONVE L–1* were implemented in 1988 followed by *PROCONVEL–2* which phased in over 1992–1996. These two standards only covered passenger vehicles. In Phase 1, control of evaporative emissions started while Phase 2 necessitated application of new technologies such as electronic fuel injection and catalytic converters to cut down emissions.
- An important step in the development of PROCONVE occurred in 1993 when all the standards were transformed into *Law No. 8.723/93* in October 1993. This federal law provides for the reduction of emission from vehicles and gives additional measures. It prescribed limits on exhaust pollutants for vehicles in different segments from January 1997. Table 4.11 lists the limits placed in emission standards after implementation of this law.
- *PROCONVE L–3* emission regulations were adopted in 1993 and implemented from 1997 to 2004. This standard was based on the Euro 2 standard with some elements drawn from the earlier Euro 1 standard.
- *PROCONVE L–4 and L–5* standards resulted from *CONAMA 315/2002* and were adopted together in the year 2002, with implementation dates ranging between 2006 and 2009. These standards were based on Euro 3 and Euro 4, respectively. PROCONVE L–4 was implemented in three phases: 40% coverage by 2005, 70% by 2006, and finally 100% by 2007. PROCONVE L–5 was implemented in 2009. Additionally, requirements for on-board diagnostics (OBD) were adopted in 2004 under *CONAMA 354/2004* for vehicles manufactured in Brazil as well as commercial vehicles imported from abroad, which followed Otto cycle.
- Finally, *CONAMA 415/2009* paved the way for the latest regulation *PROCONVE–6* which was phased in 2013 for diesel-run vehicles, in 2014 for new model gasoline-run vehicles and, finally, full coverage for gasoline-run vehicles by 2015.
- IBAMA also regulated conventional pollutant emission limits from heavy-duty vehicles. The vehicular emission program for heavy-duty vehicles is termed *PROCONVE P* in which the limits follow the European precedent. *Resolution CONAMA 18/1986* established *PROCONVE P–1* voluntary standard that was drafted in 1987 as pilot regulation for urban buses to control smoke (i.e., particulate matter) and implemented in 1990. Opacity limit (kg 2.5) was adopted throughout the maximum torque curve of diesel engines and then expanded for all heavy-duty vehicles by 1989.

[8]Curb weight refers to the cumulative weight of the vehicle with all standard equipment, full fuel tank but without any cargo or passengers. Gross vehicle weight (GVW) refers to the vehicle's curb weight plus the weight of additional accessories, cargo, and passengers.

Table 4.11 Brazilian emission norms

Standard	Year	Idle CO[a]	CO	THC	NMHC	NO*x*	HCO	PM
Passenger vehicles								
L–4	2007	0.50	2.0	0.30	0.16	0.25[b]/0.60[c]	0.03	0.05
L–5	2009[d]	0.50	2.0	0.30	0.05	0.12[b]/0.25[c]	0.03	0.05
L–6	2013[e]	0.20	1.3	0.30	0.05	0.25/0.08	0.02	0.025
Light commercial vehicles (GVW < 1700 kg)								
L–4	2007	0.50	2.0	0.30	0.16	0.25[b]/0.60[c]	0.03	0.08
L–5	2009[d]	0.50	2.0	0.30	0.05	0.12[b]/0.25[c]	0.02	0.05
L–6	2013[e]	0.20	1.3	0.30	0.05	0.08	0.02	0.03
Light commercial vehicles (GVW > 1700 kg)								
L–4	2007	0.50	2.7	0.50	0.20	0.43[b]/1.00[c]	0.06	0.10
L–5	2009[d]	0.50	2.7	0.50	0.06	0.25[b]/0.43[c]	0.04	0.06
L–6	2013[e]	0.20	2.0	0.50	0.06	0.25[b]/0.35[c]	0.03	0.04

CO carbon monoxide, *THC* total hydrocarbons, *NMHC* non-methane hydrocarbons, NO_x nitrous oxide, *HCO* aldehydes, *PM* particulate matter. Idle CO emissions measured in % volume, others measured in grams per kilometer. Vehicles in all three categories are of durability of 80,000 km/ 5 years and tested on federal test procedure (FTP-75), which is defined by the USEPA to measure tail pipe emissions of passenger cars for city driving cycle

[a]Idle CO limits apply to Otto cycle engines only, while THC limits apply only to natural gas vehicles

[b]Otto cycle engines

[c]Diesel cycle engines

[d]These standards were never implemented for diesel vehicles due to lack of low sulfur fuel in Brazil

[e]Applicable to all diesel vehicles

- *Resolution CONAMA 315/2002* established *PROCONVEP–5*, which was the equivalent of Euro III, was gradually brought in over 2004 and 2006 and introduced the transient testing method. By 2004, it covered all urban buses and a year later 40% of all heavy vehicles in the country. By the year 2006, almost all heavy-duty vehicles plying in Brazil were P–5 compliant. The same resolution also established *PROCONVE P–5* which was the equivalent of Euro IV. However, the P–6 standard, such as L–5, could never be implemented because ultralow sulfur diesel needed was not available. This is the reason why P–6 standard continued till the year 2011 to ensure sufficient demand for the fuel was met. According to the Brazilian Vehicle Manufacturers Association (ANFAVEA), to avoid serious legal consequences, the vehicle manufacturers and fuel producers had to sign a judicial commitment to pay for environmental reparatory measures.

- Finally, *Resolution CONAMA 403/2008* set forth *PROCONVEP–7* was based on Euro V emission standard. By 2012, all heavy vehicles were made P–7 compliant. Table 4.11 lists emission norms in Brazil for passenger vehicles and light commercial vehicles from 2007.

Brazil has a long history of production and use of biofuel. It is one of the largest producers and exporters of ethanol. Brazil produces this fuel additive. Fuel quality standards are regulated by the National Agency of Petroleum, Natural Gas and Biofuels (ANP–Agência Nacional do Petróleo, Gás Naturale Biocombust´ıveis) of Brazil.

References

An, F., & Sauer, A. (2004). *Comparison of passenger vehicle fuel economy and GHG emission standards around the world*. World Resources Institute, December.

Baumol, W. J., & Oates, W. E. (1971). The use of standards and prices for protection of the environment. *Swedish Journal of Economics, 73*(1), 42–54.

CPCB. (2010). *Status of the Vehicular Pollution Control Programme in India*. Ministry of Environment & Forests, Government of India, New Delhi.

Cropper, M., & Oates, W. (1992). Environmental economics: A survey. *Journal of Economic Literature, 30*(2), 675–740.

EPB. (2002). *Strengthening vehicle inspection and maintenance*. Multi-sectoral Action Plan Group, Environmental Protection Bureau of Chongqing, July 2002, PR of China.

Faiz, A., Weaver, C., & Walsh, M. (1996). *Air Pollution from Motor Vehicles, Standards and Technologies for Controlling Emissions*, Washington DC: The World Bank.

IBAMA. (2011). Air Pollution Control Program by Motor Vehicles, Proconve and Promot. Environmental Collection 3rd edition, Guideline Series—Environmental Management No. 3, Ministry of Environment, Brasilia.

Jaffe, A., Newell, R., & Stavins, R. (2005). A tale of two market failures: Technology and environmental policy. *Ecological Economics, 54*, 164–174.

Kathuria, V. (2002). *Vehicular Pollution Control in Delhi*, India. Transportation Research, Part D, *7*(5): 373–87.

Kolstad, C. D., Ulen, T. S., & Johnson, G. V. (1990). Ex post liability for Harm vs. ex ante safety regulation: Substitutes or complements? *American Economic Review, 80*, 888–901.

MEP. (2010). China Vehicle Emission Control Annual Report 2010, Ministry of Environmental Protection of the Peoples Republic of China, Beijing.

MoEF. (2010). *India: Greenhouse Gas Emissions 2007*. INCCA Indian Network for Climate Change Assessment, MoEF, Government of India.

Nelissen, D., & Requate T. (2004). *Pollution-reducing and resource-saving technological progress*. Christian-Albrechts-Universitat Kiel, Working Paper No. 2004-07.

OECD. (1997). *Evaluating economic instruments for environmental policy*. Paris: OECD.

Pandey, K., David, W., Ostro,B., Deichmann, U.,Hamilton,L., & Bolt, K. (2006). *Ambient Particulate Matter Concentrations in Residential and Pollution Hotspot Areas of World Cities: New Estimates Based on the Global Model of Ambient Particulates (GMAPS)*, Development Research Group and Environment Department, Washington D.C: World Bank

Schmitz, P. W. (2000). On the joint use of liability and safety regulation. *International Review of Law and Economics, 20*(3), 371–382.

Shavell, S. (1984). A model of the optimal use of liability and safety regulation. *Rand Journal of Economics, 15*, 271–280.

UNESCAP. (2011). *Review of developments in transport in Asia and the Pacific transport division of ESCAP*. Thailand: United Nations.

Chapter 5
Where Do Brazil, India, and China Stand?

Abstract This chapter explores the technical aspects of green technologies that are being developed to mitigate the challenges posed by vehicular pollution and fuel consumption. The use of standardized International Patent Classification (IPC) system of technologies is described to get a better understanding of the underlying green technologies. This is followed by an exercise that matches pollutants targeted in the regulations with selected patent-technology classes to develop a composite regulatory stringency index for Germany, India, Brazil, and China. The construction of a regulatory stringency index for each country builds on the information gathered in the fieldwork where interactions with technicians, industry representatives, government officials, and academicians were held.

5.1 Introduction

The term "technology-forcing standard" was perhaps first used in the 1970 US Clean Air Act leading to the development of catalytic converter technology for automobiles. Discussing the history of California's technology-forcing regulations, Miller and Solomon (2009) suggest that technology-forcing mandates with the objective of advancement in vehicular technologies branched out of technology-following policies that have reached evolutionary dead ends (p. 8).

Nentjes et al. (2007) give a theoretical focus of technology-forcing regulations on environmental policymaking. They suggested that stricter performance standards, especially technology-forcing, have the most direct and biggest impact on stimulating innovation because these standards demand higher rates of emission reduction than what is possible using the currently available off-the-shelf technologies.

Recently, the International Energy Agency proposed that technology-forcing standards are efficiency performance levels (or technology) that are currently not in the market and are too costly at present to be widespread; which require innovation and/or broad diffusion of technologies in the market; and are delivered to the market via government signaling future regulation (IEA 2012, p.9). Engine technologies are undergoing significant changes to keep up with the regulatory, fuel, and market

A. Bharadwaj, *Environmental Regulations and Innovation in Advanced Automobile Technologies*, SpringerBriefs in Economics,
https://doi.org/10.1007/978-981-10-6952-9_5

requirements. With increased competition from the emerging hybrid and electric counterparts, the traditional gasoline and diesel technologies are rapidly advancing ahead.

5.2 Technical Background

In this section, a detailed explanation of the relevant technological classes is provided. First, a description of the different technological areas associated with the relevant patent class is given, followed by examples of some patent documents which illustrate the methodology which will be used to create the regulatory stringency index in the subsequent section.

The focus of the study will be on technologies that are primarily for improvement of the internal combustion engine in terms of reducing emissions of different pollutants and saving consumption of fuel. This reflects the fact that these conventional engines are expected to dominate the light and heavy vehicle automobile segment, at least in the medium term, even if they are used together with the non-conventional electric, hybrid, plug-in hybrid, fuel cell, and hydrogen vehicular technologies.

The starting point is the selection of International Patent Classifications (IPCs) that specifically categorize emission-reducing and fuel-saving technologies. These technologies will collectively be referred as the green automotive technologies. This classification is derived from OECD (2004, 2009a) and US DOE (2011) and is discussed below. The search for green technologies was restricted to all patents that cite one of the IPC codes listed in the OECD (2009b) study.

IPC is a system used in the patent world to classify technical subject matter (such as the patent literature) and is particularly adapted for needs of patent documentation. It contains a large set of alphanumeric codes that are used to order the underlying inventions in patent applications by predetermined criteria.[1] In this study, codes up to the fourth level (subclass level) in the IPC hierarchical structure are used. This methodology has been used by a 2011 US DOE study on linking vehicular technologies in advanced combustion to more efficient, cleaner-burning engines. The tables below list the patent classes for green automotive technologies.

Some of the new diesel engine technologies for light-duty vehicles (mainly passenger and light commercial) include advanced fuel injection technologies, EGR (exhaust gas recirculation) control, advanced and two-stage turbo-charging, variable valve actuation, closed-loop combustion control, and OBD. For heavy-duty (diesel) commercial vehicles, technological advances are aimed at improving fuel economy, reliability, and durability of the engine. European regulations have

[1]The European Council initiated work in IPC in 1956, which resulted in the first edition of the system coming into force in 1968. Currently, the World Intellectual Property Organization (WIPO) maintains and administers the IPC system based on the 1971 Strasbourg Agreement. More than 100 countries, including more than 120 PCT members, apply this system. This study is based on the eighth edition of the system, IPC-8, which was introduced in 2006.

promulgated the adoption of SCR technology and, later on, EGR, DPF, and turbo-charging concepts.

Apart from exhaust emissions, automotive technologies control evaporative emissions (mainly variants of hydrocarbons like THC and NMHC), which are let out into the air through the evaporation of fuel from the vehicle. More importantly, since it affects the fuel use (economy) of the vehicle, it has serious ramifications for the overall fuel demand. This can be triggered by: (1) diurnal evaporation (from increase in outside temperature) heating the fuel tank, (2) running losses (excessively hot engine vaporizing fuel) and hot soak.

An essential element of emission reduction is the optimal management of cold start and the catalytic systems. However, the temperature of the recuperative exhaust gas has been falling over the years with turbo-charging (in gasoline engines) and increased combustion efficiency (in diesel engines). To bring emissions down, the exhaust gas temperature has to be manually increased in an efficient way to meet emission targets as well as not minimizing fuel consumption. The electrically heated catalyst (EHC) was developed precisely for the purpose of efficiently warming up the catalytic converter to meet these twin goals (Presti and Pace 2011).

Further, strict emission reduction is being made possible in a cost-effective way with use of substrate technology. The newly developed advanced metallic substrates were found to be advantageous over the standard substrates. These advanced and more complex technologies were cost-effective solutions with comparable (or better) emission efficiency for both current and future stringent emission limits, particularly NO_x (Pace and Presti 2010).

Fuel injection systems squirt atomized fuel into the engine's cylinders via spraying injectors (single or multinozzle). High sulfur content in gasoline fuel can completely cancel out any fuel savings from using advanced injectors in the gasoline-run direct injection systems. The common rail technology directly injects the right fuel into the combustion chamber at electronically controlled ultra-high pressure and, on the other hand, has made the diesel engines cleaner (lower CO_2, PM, and NO_x), more efficient (lower fuel consumption), and powerful. The main components of an electronically controlled fuel injection are: (1) the engine control unit (ECU), (2) sensors, and (3) fuel injectors. The injectors are broadly divided into two new technologies—multipoint (MPFI) and gasoline direct (GDI).

To calculate the stringency of regulations, the above IPCs are matched with the elements of environmental regulations detailed in the previous chapter. Specifically, all regulated substances in successive emission standards adopted by countries in the last two decades are matched with the six green technology classes over time. This is elaborated in the next section.

5.3 International Patent Classification for Green Automotive Technologies

See Tables 5.1, 5.2, 5.3, 5.4, 5.5, and 5.6.

Table 5.1 International Patent Classification (IPC): Technology Area B01D

Divisional	Layout	Description
Section	B	Performing operation: transporting
Subsection	B0	Separating, mixing
Class	B01	Physical or chemical processes or apparatus in general
Subclass	B01D	Separation (evaporation, distillation, crystallization, absorption, adsorption)
Group	B01D53	Separation of gases or vapors; recovering vapors of volatile solvents from gases; chemical or biological purification of waste gases, e.g., engine exhaust gases, smoke fumes, flue gases, or aerosols
Subgroup	B01D 53/92-96	(…) of engine exhaust gases (exhaust apparatus) having means for purifying or otherwise treating exhaust gases (by catalytic processes); regeneration, reactivation, or recycling of reactants

Postcombustion technologies, which include catalytic converters, lean NO_x catalysts, NO_x absorbers, catalytic regeneration devices, etc.

Table 5.2 International Patent Classification (IPC): Technology Area B01J

Divisional	Layout	Description
Section	B	Performing operation: transporting
Subsection	B0	Separating, mixing
Class	B01	Physical or chemical processes or apparatus in general
Subclass	B01J	Chemical or physical processes, e.g., catalysis, colloid chemistry; and their relevant apparatus
Group	B01J23	(…) containing catalysts comprising metals, metal oxides, hydroxides
Subgroup	B01J23/40-46	(…) Platinum group metals such as platinum, palladium, ruthenium, rhodium, osmium, or iridium

Postcombustion technologies, which include catalytic converters, lean No_x catalysts, No_x absorbers, catalytic regeneration devices, etc.

Table 5.3 International Patent Classification (IPC): Technology Area F01M

Divisional	Layout	Description
Section	F	Mechanical engineering: lighting; heating; weapons; blasting: transporting
Subsection	F0	Engines or pumps
Class	F01	Machines or engines in general; engine plants in general; steam engines
Subclass	F01M	Lubricating of machines or engines in general; lubricating internal combustion engines; crankcase ventilating
Group	F01M13	Crankcase ventilating or breathing
Subgroup	F01M 13/04	(…) Having means for purifying air before leaving crankcase, e.g., removing oil

Integrated technologies of improved engine design or engine redesign, which includes crankcase emissions and control

Table 5.4 International Patent Classification (IPC): Technology Area F02M

Divisional	Layout	Description
Section	F	Mechanical engineering: lighting; heating; weapons; blasting: transporting
Subsection	F0	Engines or pumps
Class	F02	Machines or engines in general; engine plants in general; steam engines
Subclass	F02M	Supplying combustion engines in general with combustible mixtures
Group	F02M3	Idling devices: carburetors
Group	F02M23	Apparatus for adding secondary air to fuel-air mixture
Group	F02M25	Engine-pertinent apparatus for adding non-fuel substances to combustion-air, main fuel, or fuel-air mixture
Group	F02M39-71	Arrangement of different types of fuel injection apparatus and systems with varying number and types of injectors
Subgroup	F02M 3/00-04	(…) preventing flow of idling fuel

Air-to-fuel ratio devices, fuel injection systems, electronic control systems

Table 5.5 International Patent Classification (IPC): Technology Area F01N

Divisional	Layout	Description
Section	F	Mechanical engineering: lighting; heating; weapons; blasting: transporting
Subsection	F0	Engines or pumps
Class	F01	Machines or engines in general; engine plants in general; steam engines
Subclass	F01N	Gas-flow silencers or exhaust apparatus for machines or engines in general; gas-flow silencers or exhaust apparatus for internal combustion engines
Group	F01N3	Exhaust apparatus having means for purifying, rendering innocuous, or otherwise treating exhaust
Group	F01N5	Exhaust apparatus combined or associated With devices profiting by exhaust energy
Group	F01N9	Electric control of exhaust gas treating apparatus
Group	F01N11	Monitoring or diagnostic devices for exhaust gas treatment apparatus
Subgroup	F01N 3/05,08-34	(…) by means of inertial or centrifugal separators for rendering innocuous; by thermal or catalytic conversion of noxious components of exhaust.
Subgroup	F01N5/00+	(…) the devices using heat or kinetic energy
Subgroup	F01N 9/00+	
Subgroup	F01N 11/00+	Constructional features of exhaust apparatus arrangement

Integrated technologies of improved engine design or engine redesign which includes crankcase emissions and control, air-to-fuel ratio devices, catalytic converters, EGR valves, electronic control systems and plasma-based technologies, and oxygen, NO_x, and temperature sensors

Table 5.6 International Patent Classification (IPC): Technology Area F02D

Divisional	Layout	Description
Section	F	Mechanical engineering: lighting; heating; weapons; blasting: transporting
Subsection	F0	Engines or pumps
Class	F02	Physical or chemical processes or apparatus In general
Subclass	F02D	Controlling combustion engines
Group	F02D41	Electric control of supply of combustible mix or its constituents
Group	F02D43	Conjoint electrical control, e.g., ignition, fuel-air mixture, recirculation, supercharging, exhaust gas treatment
Group	F02D45	Electric control of supply of combustible mix or its constituents
Subgroup	F02D 41/00+	(…) circuit arrangements for generating control signals; for engine starting or for idling
Subgroup	F02D41/14	Electrical control not provided in other groups
Subgroup	F02D 43/00+	(…) analog or digital means
Subgroup	F02D 45/00+	

Electronic control systems and plasma-based technologies, and oxygen, NO_x, and temperature sensors

5.4 Matching Regulations with IPCs

In Europe, the regulation under study, Directive 70/220/EEC, is the primal environmental regulation for the transport sector. It was amended 120 times between 1988 and 2011 out of which 37 amendments relate to emissions and fuel consumption of vehicles. This regulation also served as the guiding pillar for subsequent regulations framed in India, China, and Brazil. Most recently, in 2013, three legislations were adopted in Europe pertaining to emissions and fuel consumption in motor vehicles.

A time line of the 37 relevant regulations covered by the amendments is presented in Table 5.7. To construct the stringency index, these amendments were individually analyzed and matched with the technology classes.

The first amendment, for instance, was made on June 16, 1988 under the Council Directive 88/436/EEC on the approximation of the laws of the Member States relating to measures to be taken against air pollution by gases from engines of motor vehicles, specifically restrictions of particulate pollutant emissions from diesel engines. It states: Section 3.1: *The application for approval of a vehicle type with regard to the emission of gaseous and particulate pollutants from its engine is submitted by the vehicle manufacturer or by his authorized representative*. The first sentence now reads as follows: *3.1 The components liable to affect the emission of gaseous and particulate pollutants must be so designed, constructed and assembled as to enable the vehicle, in normal use, to comply with the requirements of this Directive.*

Table 5.7 List of relevant amendments to European Directive 70/220/EEC

Year	Amendments
1988	Council Directive 88/436/EEC; Council Directive 88/77/EEC; Council Directive 88/76/EEC
1989	Council Directive 89/458/EEC
1991	Council Directive 91/542/EEC; Council Directive 91/441/EEC
1993	Commission Directive 93/116/EC; Council Directive 93/59/EEC
1994	Directive 94/12/EC of the European Parliament and the Council
1996	Directive 96/69/EC; Commission Directive 96/44/EC
1997	Commission Directive 97/20/EC
1998	Commission Directive 98/77/EC; Directive 98/69/EC
1999	Commission Directive 1999/102/EC; Commission Directive 1999/100/EC; Directive 1999/96/EC
2001	Directive 2001/100/EC; Commission Directive 2001/27/EC; Directive 2001/1/EC
2002	Commission Directive 2002/80/EC
2003	Commission Directive 2003/76/EC
2004	Directive 2004/3/EC of the European Parliament and of the Council
2005	Commission Directive 2005/78/EC; Directive 2005/55/EC; Commission Directive 2005/21/EC
2006	Commission Directive 2006/51/EC; Directive 2006/40/EC
2007	Regulation (EC) No. 7 15/2007 of The European Parliament and of the Council; Commission Directive 2007/34/EC
2008	Commission Regulation (EC) No 692/2008; Commission Directive 2008/74/EC
2009	Regulation (EC) No. 595/2009; Regulation (EC) No. 79/2009
2010	Commission Regulation (EU) No. 406/2010
2011	Commission Regulation (EU) No. 582/2011

To get a better understanding of the specifics of regulations, the following section provides examples of pollutants (covered in regulations) and how they are tackled with technological adjustments. The emission limits on these substances were increasingly tightened with successive regulations. For example, the technology-forcing regulation to introduce catalytic converters is linked to B01D and F01N technology areas, which relate to postcombustion technologies to reduce NOx emissions; fuel economy regulations are linked to F02M which relates to fuel injection systems.[2] The emission regulations prescribe specific limits on key pollutants some of which are explained below.

- Nitrogen oxides (NO_x) are formed during the combustion process in which nitrogen in the air and in the fuel is burned in the process. The temperatures

[2]Several regulations such as sound limit, criteria for wheels, and braking systems are not taken into account because they do not directly affect emission control technologies. Experts were consulted to understand the linkages between specific technologies and specific pollutants the emission regulations seek to control.

during the combustion in engines that run on diesel fuel are much higher compared to gasoline, and therefore generate much more quantity of this harmful pollutant. For reduction of NO_x emissions, the following technologies have proved to be effective—(1) SCR, selective catalytic reduction (with ammonia resulting from urea injection and decomposition in the exhaust), (2) NO_x absorbing materials that store NO_x and release them under appropriate (for the reduction of NO_x to nitrogen) conditions in the exhaust, and (3) selective NO_x reduction with the aid of HCs. For carbon monoxide and hydrocarbons, on the one hand, diesel oxidation catalysts (DOCs) are used for oxidation of gases to carbon dioxide. Soot emission, on the other hand, is reduced by employing diesel particulate filter (DPFs).

- Hydrocarbon (HC) emissions result when fuel molecules in the engine do not burn or burn only partially. They react with sunlight to form ground-level ozone, which is a major component of smog. Joergl et al. (2008) discussed the effects of various diesel oxidization catalyst designs on HC and CO tailpipe emissions, on fuel economy, and on the overall performance of the modern diesel engines. Their work threw light on the unconcluded discussion on choosing whether to reduce NO_x through internal engine techniques (such as EGR or variable valve timing) or through exhaust after-treatment devices (such as absorbers or SCR systems). They compared Euro 4 compliant technologies (such as the old diesel oxidization catalyst (DOC) and common rail fuel injection (CRDI) technologies to control tailpipe HC and CO emissions) with the new Euro 5 compliant technologies (with more stable catalyst coatings which lower the precious metal costs of the DOC) such as the coated wall flow diesel particulate filters.
- Carbon monoxide (CO) is a colorless, odorless, and poisonous gas. It results from incomplete combustion of hydrocarbon-based fuels such as gasoline or diesel in the engine and is emitted directly from the tailpipe of the vehicle. Inhalation of this gas can have severe ramifications on human health if it enters the bloodstream. Oxidization catalysts are advanced retrofit variants of two-way catalysts (for gasoline engines) which are now used to oxidize hydrocarbons and CO as well as reduce PM in diesel engines. Catalytic converter technology—designed to convert carbon monoxide to carbon dioxide—was equipped in most cars since 1980s in Germany and 1990s in India, China, and Brazil. To optimize efficiency of these converters, manufacturers introduced supplementary technologies such as onboard computers and oxygen sensors. CO emissions tend to increase dramatically in cold weather because vehicles need more fuel for ignition and the cold temperatures reduce the efficiency of converters and sensors. Another way to reduce CO emissions is to add oxygen-containing compounds such as alcohols to gasoline to achieve complete combustion by leaning out the air-to-fuel ratio.
- Particulate Matter (PM) is fine particle that is formed during the combustion and from mixing of different pollutants in the air. Diesel-run vehicles also emit more PM than gasoline counterparts. Emissions emanating from the gasoline engines (stoichiometric) have come down significantly in the last decade particularly because of the wide use of three-way catalytic converter technology. Much

attention and thought is being put into reducing diesel emissions. Emission control technologies to reduce PM include diesel oxidation catalysts (DOCs), diesel particulate filters (DPFs), and closed crankcase ventilation (CCV). Emission control technologies to reduce NO_x include exhaust gas recirculation (EGR), selective catalytic reduction (SCR), lean NO_x catalysts (LNCs), and lean NO_x traps (LNTs). Along with oxidization catalysts, diesel particulate filters are also retrofit devices highly popular in Europe and lately in heavy-duty trucks in the USA. These filters primarily achieve reduction in PM by trapping superfine and submicron particles that can cause severe respiratory problems. Exhaust gas recirculation (EGR) technology is touted as the most effective technology to minimize noxious nitrogen emissions.

- Sulfur dioxide (SO_2) occurs when the fuel used in the vehicles contain sulfur additives. Since diesel fuel contains much more quantity of sulfur than gasoline, it also emits more of this pollutant.
- Volatile organic compounds (VOCs) are carbon-based compounds that are part of the exhaust emission (from incomplete combustion) and evaporation of fuel (tank refueling). Because of the lower temperature of combustion and greater volatility, gasoline engines emit more CO and VOCs than diesel engines.

5.5 Findings: Regulatory Stringency Index

Based on the matching of regulatory interventions with IPC technology classes based on individual pollutants restricted in all the implemented emission norms, this section presents the regulatory stringency index for Germany, India, Brazil, and China. The tables below report the cumulative index of regulatory stringency that will be used for the subsequent empirical analysis. The baseline index shows the distribution of regulations restricting the pollutants over time and across the green IPC classes of emission-reducing and fuel-saving technologies.

5.5.1 Germany

European directive 70/220/EEC and all amendments from 1987 to 2011 were linked with the six key green technology classes. Each pollutant covered in the amendments was taken into consideration, and the underlying technologies to limit that pollutant were considered for the matching.

No sudden jump in stringency is observed in Germany during 1987–2011 but multiple, albeit modest, jumps can be seen occurring at almost regular intervals implying increasing stringency of environmental regulations to reduce vehicular emissions and fuel consumption (Fig. 5.1; Table 5.8).

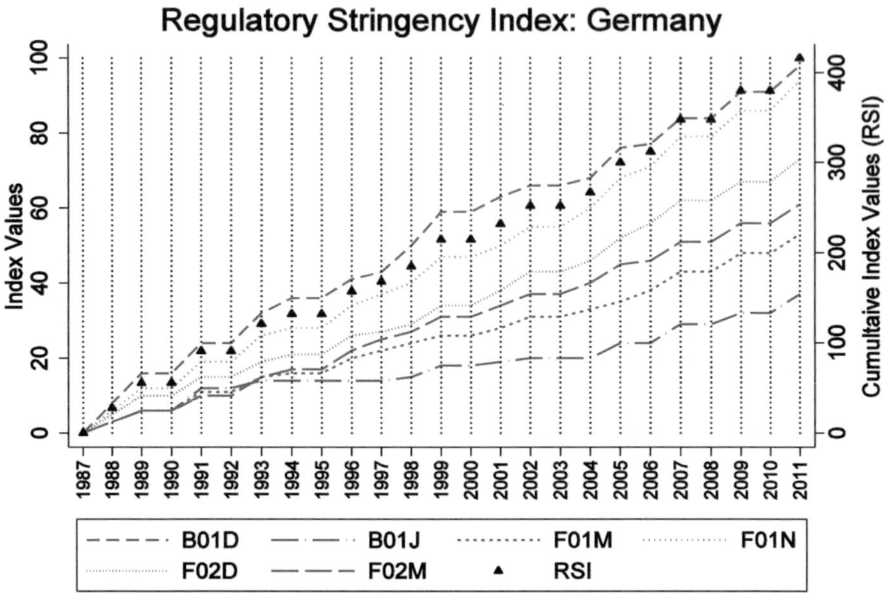

Fig. 5.1 Regulatory Stringency Index of Germany

5.5.2 *India*

The Indian Motor Vehicles Act of 1988 (MVA) and the Central Motor Vehicles Rules of 1989 (CMVR) are the principal instruments governing the emission norms and safety standards pertaining to motor vehicles in India. Since the implementation of idle emission standards in 1991, India has introduced seven successively stricter environmental regulations to curb emissions and enhance fuel economy between 1991 and 2010. In contrast to the German case, stringency of Indian regulations was increased step wise, which is reflected in the jumps in the graph (Fig. 5.2).

Contrary to popular belief, India, just like China and Brazil, does not blindly emulate Euro norms but dons a variant of Bharat Stage (BS) emission norms. They are tailored to suit specific needs and demands of Indian conditions. The difference between, say Euro II/III and BS-II/III, norms essentially lie in environmental needs, geographical needs, and testing procedures. The testing for Euro norms is done at subzero temperatures in European countries, which, without changes, is unsuitable and inappropriate for Indian conditions where the average temperature ranges between 24 and 28 °C. The norms also differ in terms of the maximum speed at which the motor vehicles are tested. At a given emission level, the BS-III stipulates 90 kmph compared to 120 kmph for Euro III (Table 5.9).[3]

[3]In addition, the test measurement on chassis dynamometer in Europe requires a weight load of 100 kg in another wise unloaded car. In India, the equivalent norms mandate a weight load of 150 kg to achieve the desired inertia weight because of differing road conditions.

Table 5.8 Cumulative Regulatory Stringency Index (RSI): Germany

Year	B01D	B01J	F01M	F01N	F02D	F02M	RSI
1987	0	0	0	0	0	0	0
1988	8	3	3	6	5	3	28
1989	16	6	6	12	10	6	56
1990	16	6	6	12	10	6	56
1991	24	12	11	19	15	10	91
1992	24	12	11	19	15	10	91
1993	32	14	15	26	19	15	121
1994	36	14	16	28	21	17	132
1995	36	14	16	28	21	17	132
1996	41	14	20	34	26	22	157
1997	43	14	22	37	27	25	168
1998	50	15	24	40	29	27	185
1999	59	18	26	47	34	31	215
2000	59	18	26	47	34	31	215
2001	63	19	28	50	38	34	232
2002	66	20	31	55	43	37	252
2003	66	20	31	55	43	37	252
2004	68	20	33	60	46	40	267
2005	76	24	35	68	52	45	300
2006	77	24	38	71	56	46	312
2007	84	29	43	79	62	51	348
2008	84	29	43	79	62	51	348
2009	91	32	48	86	67	56	380
2010	91	32	48	86	67	56	380
2011	98	37	53	94	73	61	416

5.5.3 China

The Law of the People's Republic of China on the "Prevention and Control of Atmospheric Pollution" (simplified as "Air Pollution Law") is the principal legal basis for developing motor vehicle environmental compliance management in China. The law was adopted by the Standing Committee of the National People's Congress in 1987 and was revised successively in 1995 and 2000.

These efforts led to the adoption of Euro 1 equivalent emission norms in 1999, which is also the first big jump in the regulatory stringency index. The three successively stricter regulations in the years 2002, 2005, and 2007, brought China closer to the German regulatory stringency level.

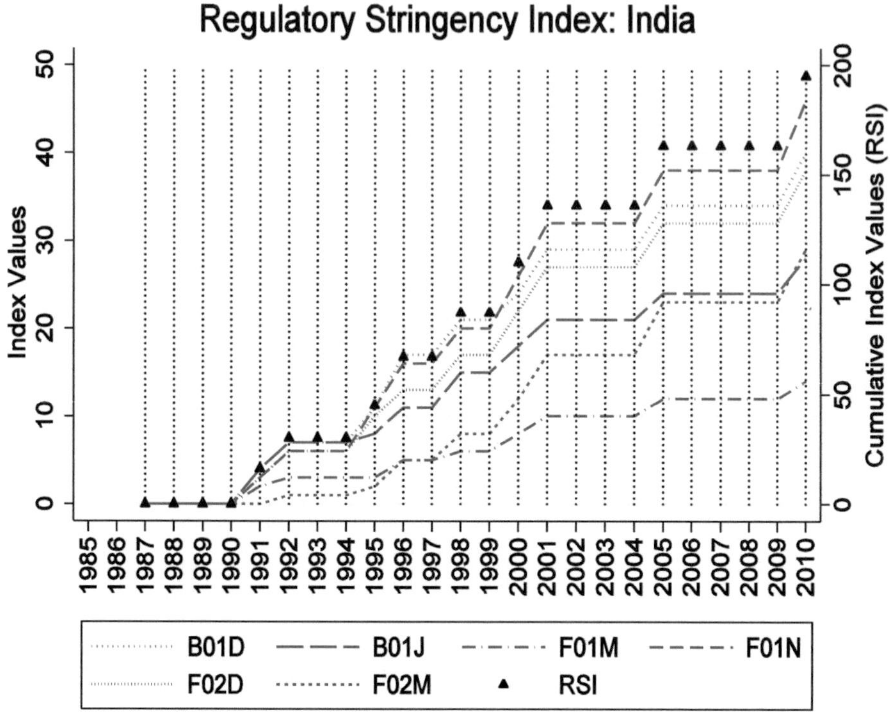

Fig. 5.2 Regulatory Stringency Index of India

5.5.4 *Brazil*

CONAMA Resolution No. 18/1986 states that:

> (…) emission of pollutants by motor vehicles contributes to the continuing deterioration of air quality, especially in urban centers; the use of appropriate technologies, of proven use, allows the response to the needs of pollution control, as well as fuel saving; the needs of time, for technological adjustment of new engines and vehicles to the pollution control requirements, resolves to establish, on a national basis, the Air Pollution Control Program by Motor Vehicles (PROCONVE), with the objective to reduce the emission levels of pollutants by motor vehicles in order to meet the Air Quality Standards, especially in urban centers and to promote the national technological development, both in automotive engineering, and in methods and equipment for testing and measuring the emission of pollutants.

After CONAMA Resolution No. 18/1986, six more resolutions were passed until October 1993 to prescribe emission limits of which two resolutions restricted noise emission level. All these standards were transformed into Law No. 8.723/1993 in October 1993. From 1993 till July 2011, CONAMA passed thirty more resolutions. Out of these, eight resolutions focused on noise limits, procedural amendments to

Table 5.9 Cumulative Regulatory Stringency Index (RSI): India

Year	B01D	B01J	F01M	F01N	F02D	F02M	RSI
1987	0	0	0	0	0	0	0
1988	0	0	0	0	0	0	0
1989	0	0	0	0	0	0	0
1990	0	0	0	0	0	0	0
1991	4	4	2	3	3	0	16
1992	7	7	3	6	6	1	30
1993	7	7	3	6	6	1	30
1994	7	7	3	6	6	1	30
1995	11	8	3	11	10	2	45
1996	17	11	5	16	13	5	67
1997	17	11	5	16	13	5	67
1998	21	15	6	20	17	8	87
1999	21	15	6	20	17	8	87
2000	24	18	8	26	22	12	110
2001	29	21	10	32	27	17	136
2002	29	21	10	32	27	17	136
2003	29	21	10	32	27	17	136
2004	29	21	10	32	27	17	136
2005	34	24	12	38	32	23	163
2006	34	24	12	38	32	23	163
2007	34	24	12	38	32	23	163
2008	34	24	12	38	32	23	163
2009	34	24	12	38	32	23	163
2010	40	28	14	46	38	29	195

Resolution 18/1986, oil specifications, licensing requirements of new fuels, and harmonization of PROCONVE with MERCOSUR.

Further, between 1996 and 2010, the Brazilian Institute of Environment and Renewable Natural Resources (IBAMA) passed twenty additional environmental regulations for motor vehicles. Out of these, four were normative instructions and directives for vehicle inspection, maintenance, and usage of compliance seal, while the rest prescribed emission limits and fuel use.

Article 1 of the Federal Law No. 8.723/1993 states that "As an integral part of the National Environmental Policy, the engines and vehicles manufacturers and the fuels manufacturers are obligated to take the necessary measures to reduce the emission levels of carbon monoxide, nitrogen oxides, hydrocarbons, alcohols and aldehydes, soot, particulate material and other pollutant compounds in the vehicles commercialized in the country, matching them to the limits set forth in this Law and observing, also, the timeframes set forth therein."

Therefore, out of the total 56 amendments and revisions of the CONAMA Resolution No. 18/1986 and the Brazilian Law No. 8.723/1993, 42 were selected

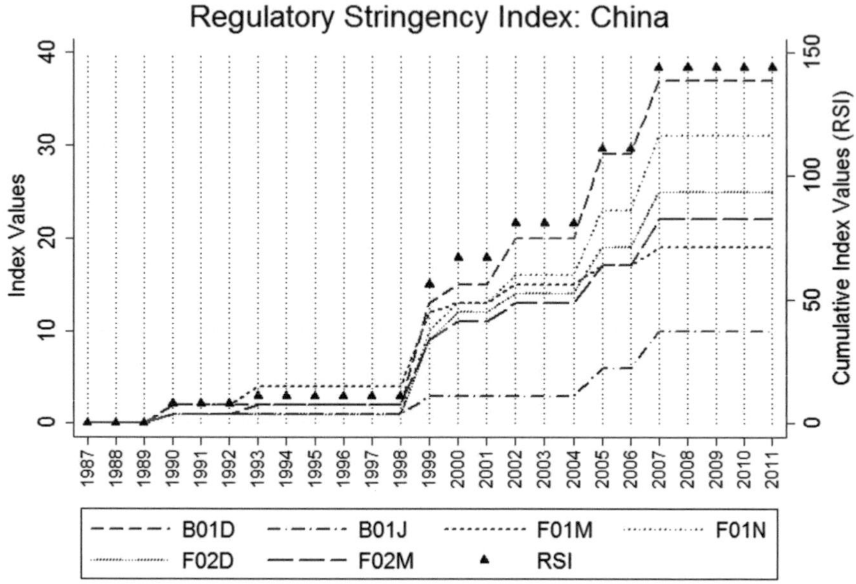

Fig. 5.3 Regulatory Stringency Index of China

because of their direct association with emission norms. Each pollutant covered in the amendments was taken into consideration, and the underlying technologies to limit that pollutant were considered for the matching with the six key green technology classes. The resulting regulatory stringency index is shown in Table 5.11. Its figure below shows five jumps in stringency of environment regulations in Brazil during 1987–2011. The years that witnessed these jumps were 1994, 1997, 1998, 2005, and 2009 (Fig. 5.4).

The existing economic literature lacks consensus on an appropriate method to quantify the strictness of environmental regulations in order to analyze the regulatory impact on different areas. The objective of creating a stringency index for environmental regulations in this chapter was to understand the evolution of regulations geared toward reducing vehicular emissions and fuel consumption and their strictness over time across Germany, India, China, and Brazil. The bases of this index were the several emission norms, fuel specifications, and technology standards implemented in each of these countries between 1987 and 2010. This index was created by carefully matching: (A) pollutants, toxins, fuel contents, and adopted technologies as covered by the regulations with (B) the technologies consolidated under the International Patent Classification system.

Table 5.10 Cumulative Regulatory Stringency Index (RSI): China

Year	B01D	B01 J	F01M	F01N	F02D	F02M	RSI
1987	0	0	0	0	0	0	0
1988	0	0	0	0	0	0	0
1989	0	0	0	0	0	0	0
1990	2	1	2	1	1	1	8
1991	2	1	2	1	1	1	8
1992	2	1	2	1	1	1	8
1993	2	1	4	1	1	2	11
1994	2	1	4	1	1	2	11
1995	2	1	4	1	1	2	11
1996	2	1	4	1	1	2	11
1997	2	1	4	1	1	2	11
1998	2	1	4	1	1	2	11
1999	13	3	12	10	9	9	56
2000	15	3	13	13	12	11	67
2001	15	3	13	13	12	11	67
2002	20	3	15	16	14	13	81
2003	20	3	15	16	14	13	81
2004	20	3	15	16	14	13	81
2005	29	6	17	23	19	17	111
2006	29	6	17	23	19	17	111
2007	37	10	19	31	25	22	144
2008	37	10	19	31	25	22	144
2009	37	10	19	31	25	22	144
2010	37	10	19	31	25	22	144
2011	37	10	19	31	25	22	144

5.6 Conclusion

The index presented in this chapter shows comparison of stringency across countries during 1987–2010 and the evolution of regulatory stringency across technology classes for each country. Being an automotive pioneer, the result that Germany's environmental regulations are most stringent is not surprising. However, the variation in evolution across the three technologically proficient developing countries is interesting. Brazil's regulatory stringency was more than that of India and China in the 1990s, and it was found that this scenario remained the same in the next decade. India managed to tighten its environmental regulations over time and outpaced China's index values.

Table 5.11 Cumulative Regulatory Stringency Index (RSI): Brazil

Year	B01D	B01J	F01M	F01 N	F02D	F02M	RSI
1987	0	0	0	0	0	0	0
1988	5	2	1	2	2	3	15
1989	9	2	2	4	3	7	27
1990	14	6	7	8	5	11	51
1991	17	6	8	9	6	13	59
1992	22	7	11	13	10	17	80
1993	22	7	11	13	10	17	80
1994	28	11	15	19	14	22	109
1995	28	11	15	19	14	22	109
1996	28	11	15	19	14	22	109
1997	34	14	20	25	18	27	138
1998	39	18	24	30	21	32	164
1999	39	18	24	30	21	32	164
2000	39	18	24	30	21	32	164
2001	40	18	24	31	21	32	166
2002	40	18	24	31	21	32	166
2003	40	18	24	31	21	32	166
2004	44	22	27	37	26	37	193
2005	52	24	32	44	31	43	226
2006	53	24	33	46	34	45	235
2007	53	24	33	46	34	45	235
2008	53	24	33	46	34	45	235
2009	62	28	38	54	39	50	271
2010	62	28	38	54	39	50	271
2011	62	28	38	54	39	50	271

No sudden jump in stringency is observed in Germany during 1987–2011 but multiple, albeit modest, jumps can be seen occurring at almost regular intervals implying increasing stringency of environmental regulations to reduce vehicular emissions and fuel consumption. Postcombustion technologies such as catalytic converters and NO_x absorbers covered in IPC B01D were found to be the most heavily regulated technology class, and it remained this way for the entire period considered. The index shows that till mid-1990s the stringency of IPC classes F02M, F01M, and B01J was not too different, but there was a divergence between them by the mid-2000s. India adopted emission and fuel regulation before China and Brazil but has been slower in their subsequent tightening.

After the initial jumps in India's regulatory stringency index during the 1990s, India implemented stricter norms only after the turn of the century in three leaps—2000, 2005, and 2010–which brought India relatively closer to the accepted standards in the industrialized world. IPC classes, F01D and B01J, which started out as the most regulated (and important in terms of emission-reducing and fuel-saving

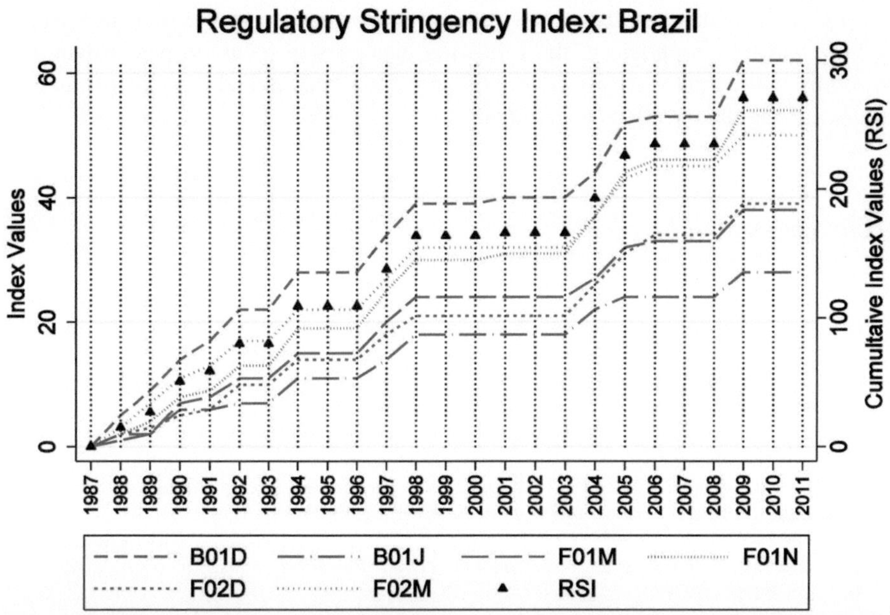

Fig. 5.4 Regulatory Stringency Index of Brazil

technologies), were overtaken by new integrated technologies of improved engine design such as better air-to-fuel ratio devices and EGR valves. The adoption of Euro 1 equivalent emission norms in China in 1999 was the first big jump in the regulatory stringency index. There were three subsequent jumps in the years 2002, 2005, and 2007, which brought China closer to the much stricter level of the German stringency index. Opting for a clear stepwise introduction of emission norms, China's regulations are now linked with IPC classes B01D and F01N more than the other classes. The regulatory stringency index of Brazil shows five jumps in stringency of environment regulations in Brazil during 1987–2011. The years that witnessed these jumps were 1994, 1997, 1998, 2005, and 2009.

This chapter explored the technical aspects of green technologies that are being developed to mitigate the challenges posed by vehicular pollution and fuel consumption. The use of standardized International Patent Classification (IPC) system of technologies was described to construct a stringency index based on classification of the patentable technologies. The chapter then provided details of key technological classes as defined under the IPC system.

This was followed by the exercise to match pollutants targeted in the regulations with the selected technological areas to develop a composite regulatory stringency index for each country. The construction of the index builds on the information gathered in the fieldwork where interactions with technicians, industry representatives, and government officials were held. It greatly facilitated the exercise to link elements of regulations with relevant technologies. The focus was specifically on the emission-reducing and fuel-saving regulatory changes in the transport sector. Having laid the groundwork, the following chapter will focus on patent data, followed by multivariate analysis where the index has been linked with the patent data to discern regulatory effect on innovation.

References

DOE. (2011). Linkages from DOEs vehicle technologies R&D in advanced combustion to more efficient, cleaner burning engines by R. Ruegg and P. Thomas, US Department of Energy, June 2009.

IEA. (2012). Technology forcing standards for energy efficiency, efficient electrical end-use equipment (4E), IEA Energy Transport Network, June 2012, Oxford.

Miller, P., & Solomon, M. (2009). A brief history of technology forcing motor vehicle regulations air and waste management association. June 2009 Issue.

Nentjes, A., de Vries, F. P., & Wiersma, D. (2007). Technology forcing through environmental regulation. *European Journal of Political Economy, 23,* 903916.

OECD. (2004). *Can cars come clean? Strategies for low-emission vehicles*. Paris: OECD.

OECD. (2009a). *Responding to the economic crisis: Fostering industrial restructuring and renewal*. Paris: OECD.

OECD. (2009b). Effects of environmental policy on the type of innovation: The case of automotive emission-control technologies In I. Hascic, F. de Vries, N. Johnstone & N. Medhi (Eds.), *OECD Journal: Economic Studies*, Vol 2009.

Pace, L., & Presti, M. (2010). Changing the substrate technology to meet future emission limits. *SAE International Journal of Fuels and Lubricants, 3*(2), 395–403.

Pace, L., & Presti, M. (2011). An alternative way to reduce fuel consumption during cold start: The electrically heated catalyst. SAE Technical Paper 2011-24-0178.

Chapter 6
Insights from the World of Patents

Abstract The previous chapter analyzed the regulations to construct a regulatory stringency index for Germany, India, China, and Brazil. This chapter introduces patent data for the four countries and explores various characteristics of the data. An illustration of patenting trends across technologies and markets is followed by a discussion of metrics of innovation highlighted in the literature. Special emphasis is given to patenting as a metric of innovation and its suitability in this study. After this, the patent data used in this study is introduced along with details of patent filings, priorities, and composition of assignees across the four countries.

6.1 Patenting Trends Across Technologies and Markets

The three emerging economies considered in this study—Brazil, India, and China (hereafter BIC) are substantially different from Germany in terms of GDP growth, growth rate of patenting in green technologies, and regulatory intervention. Countries that had, until recently, comparative advantage in labor-intensive low-technology goods and services are increasingly becoming leaders in innovation. This is particularly true in China, which has undergone significant changes in the last decade. Companies in Brazil and India are also getting more competitive and innovative not just domestically but also globally.

Patenting trends in "green" automotive technologies in these three emerging markets and Germany are presented in this chapter. Germany, because of its technological capabilities particularly in automotive engineering, has been one of the biggest creator and manufacturer of automotive technologies in the world. The other three countries have joined the race to become more technologically proficient. For instance, the growth of PCT filings between 2006 and 2011 was 33.4% in China, 13% in Brazil while India recorded a near double-digit growth. The grant of patents in Europe is administered by the EPO, which is a single destination for

A. Bharadwaj, *Environmental Regulations and Innovation in Advanced Automobile Technologies*, SpringerBriefs in Economics,
https://doi.org/10.1007/978-981-10-6952-9_6

several Member States. The descriptive patent analysis shown in this chapter investigates the nature and compositions of patenting of green automotive innovations in these four countries individually.

6.2 Measures of Innovation

There are different measures of innovation that have been relied upon in the literature. Expenditure on R&D is a widely used input measure of innovation. But, data on such expenditure, along with number of scientists and personnel involved in basic research, is not available at a disaggregated private level and is therefore not a good measure for the purpose of this study. Output of R&D is a better measure and can be of two types—scientific publications or bibliometric data and patent or technometric data. Patent data provides a good measure of the output of the innovation activity or of the inventive process (Griliches 1990) that is compiled by different countries in a standardized format.[1]

The work by Lanjouw and Mody (1996) was the first to study environmental technology in the technology pioneering countries and in a group of developing countries using patent data. Building on their work, Johnstone et al. (2010) use count of patents to investigate the impact of policies on environmental technologies in the OECD countries where patent data is more easily available and is more complete than in the developing countries. Dechezleprêtre et al. (2010) have used patent data (patent count as a proxy of innovation) across countries to study the trends in environmental technology. However, they do not include some important technology classes such as electric vehicles, energy-efficient technologies in industry or clean coal technologies (p. 9).

According to Peters and Pottelsberghe de la Potterie (2006), the debate around patent applications being a measure of innovation activity revolves around three main reasons.[2] First, the fundamental conditions of patentability-inventive step, industrial applicability, and non-obviousness, are not always met. Second, the propensity to patent technologies is variable across countries. In the automotive industry, patenting in the four sampled countries is generally high relative to other sectors. Third, in some sectors protection through patents is not always the sought after instrument.

[1]See Adams et al. (2006), Hinze and Schmoch (2004) for patents as proxy of innovation activity.

[2]See Schmookler's (1966 and 1972) pioneering work on the use of patent statistics, Scherer's acclaimed 1965 work on innovation using patent data and Griliches's (1990) work on the use of patent statistics as economic indicators.

In the automotive sector, protection of inventions through patents is generally the preferred instrument compared to other mechanisms (such as secrecy). However, mechanisms such as lead-time and technological complexity also tend to complement the efficiency of patent protection measure. Therefore, patenting can be considered as the best option available to legally protect the invention of (complex) automotive technologies from imitation and/or introduction of products incorporating reverse engineered technologies.

One type of indicator used in this study is the count of the number of patents applied for in a country. Propensity to patent tends to be higher in technologically advanced countries, such as Germany, and it is typically lower in developing countries. The three other countries chosen in this study, even though developing, are more technologically proficient than other countries in their respective cohort. Another type of measure used in the study is the count of patent applications weighted by the relevant IPC codes. Here, the total number of IPCs assigned in each patent application (including the six core IPCs) was taken into account.

6.3 Data and Sources

Collection of data and information was carried out using a three-pronged strategy through publicly and privately available online patent data, information directly from patent offices and interviews conducted with representatives of the automotive industry as well as government officials. For the purpose of studying technological innovation in environment-friendly technologies, patent data has become increasingly popular.

This study follows the example of the other contributions in this field to examine the links between environmental policy and innovation. Patent data has various advantages in this context. They provide detailed information about the invention. The availability of detailed patent classifications can be used to identify the relevant field of technology and link particular inventions to regulatory measures. Patents were extracted by technology class and priority year. The latter is preferable because it is the best available approximation of the date of invention.

All patent filings in Germany and BIC, identified by the IPC codes discussed in the previous chapter, from 1985 until 2011, were extracted. The data was accessed from PATSAT (version 2013). EPO's World Patent Statistical Database (PATSTAT) is unique and elaborate in that it covers more than 80 patent offices and over 70 million patent documents. However, the coverage of Indian and Brazilian patent data in PATSTAT is not satisfactory. PATSTAT is based on DOCDB, the internal European Patent Office (EPO) master documentation database, where this data was found to be missing. The very simple reason is that the EPO has been struggling hard to get an electronic delivery of Indian, Brazilian, and Chinese data for few years now. Therefore, alternate reliable data sources had to be tapped to fill this gap.

To complement this data, patent information was derived from individual patent offices. In order to obtain authentic data directly from patent offices, services of Innovaccer were sought to mine patent information for India, Brazil, and China from official patent office gazettes, notification documents, online patent information retrieval systems (iPairs 2.0 for India, e-Patentes Platform for Brazil, Patent Information Service Platform for China, and EPO's Espacenet) using the relevant IPC codes. Finally, detailed interviews were carried out with automotive industry representatives and policy makers about their opinion on green technology trajectory, emission regulations, and role for technological innovation through patenting activities

All four patent offices have similar filing or priority date to publication time line, but there are numerous exceptions across countries. Further, the number of offices also varies across these countries. While Brazil has one formal PTO along with two other substantive offices, India has four PTOs and China has 3 offices taking care of patent procedures. In Europe, Munich is home not only to Germany's patent and trademark office but also to European Patent Office with its mechanical engineering branch located in this office. Patent pendency, the length of time it takes from filing to grant of a patent, also differs across countries. According to figures from Baker and McKenzie (2012), it takes approximately 2–4 years in China, 2–5 years in India and 6–8 years in Brazil for patents to be granted from filing date. The pendency period in the German Patent Office is longer due to its comparatively long, seven-year examination deferral system (Henkel and Jell 2009).

The average European patent pendency from data observed in the European Patents Bulletin in 2012 was approximately 5 years; however, several patent applications at the EPO are PCT applications, which reach the European Patent Office after 18 months from filing. If this is taken into account, then the pendency period at the EPO is between 3.5 and 4 years (James Knowles, patentia.co.uk, patent pendency I, II; 28 May 2012 and 20 June 2012). Whereas all three emerging economies (BIC) accept divisional applications, patents of addition (called continuations-in-part in the USA) are only available in India where any new material will receive a new date from the patent office. Explicit duty of candor (to disclose all prior art information relevant to the patent application) is also not available in BIC.[3]

[3]In India, the applicant must inform the office of all similar foreign patents. In China, disclosure of prior art is done at the time of making a substantive examination request, but there are no legal ramifications of not doing so.

6.4 Understanding the Dataset

This section gives an overview of "green" patent filings in Germany, India, China, and Brazil in the automotive sector. Patent data collected for these countries were aggregated and analyzed in three different ways:

(i) Patterns of patent filings and granted patents over time
(ii) Patent filings within each country and comparison across countries
(iii) Patent filings across technology classes and application.

6.4.1 *Variables and Definitions*

Information available in a patent document and patent application was carefully extracted, normalized, and coded.[4] Individual applicants and government organizations were purposefully left out in decomposing the applicants because most of the assignees in all countries were private automotive companies operating in more than one country. Information on the number and nature of all assignees in each patent application was also decomposed. In automotive industry, it is common for inventors from different companies or institutions to enter into collaborations and joint research. Several automotive companies actively fund research projects in public universities. Therefore, to get an idea of the nature of research collaborations reflected in joint applications for an invention, differences in assignees were also examined.

6.4.2 *Legal Status*

Before getting into the filing trends, we briefly see the legal status of all filings as mentioned in the patent applications. The legal status was found to be very different both within a country and across countries. Since the absolute number of applications filed in each of these countries varies substantially in all years, intra-country percentages were derived to get a perspective of the pipeline of the process post-filing. As a caveat, information on the current legal status was not available for 42% of the total number of Brazilian applications, 13% of total Indian applications, 30% of total German applications, and 2% of total Chinese patent applications.

[4]A list of keywords used to identify applicants as private companies, publicly listed companies, academic institutions, and multinational corporations is in the appendix.

In Brazil and India, almost 20% (901 and 242, respectively) of total patent applications that were filed (green technologies in the automotive industry) were granted by 2011. The number of granted patents was significantly higher in China (48% of 21,700 applicants or 10,438 number of patents). Germany, during the same period, granted 4,342 patents (9.5% of total applications). Apart from the high share of Indian applications that are still under review, the high grant rate of "green" patents in China was an interesting statistic captured in the descriptive analysis.

6.4.3 Application Fillings and Grants

The relatively low number of granted Indian patents was partly because more than 60% were still under review at the time of data collection. This reason is actually evident from the unreal figure of zero rejected applications. Comparatively, about 25% of Chinese applications and 20% of German applications were under patent review and examination process. Regarding distribution of patents that were granted till 2011, only 20% of Indian applications (189) were granted in India, while more than 90% (2808) were granted in Brazil in the same period.

Figure 6.1 shows the filing trend of "green" patents from 1980 until 2010. The graph clearly shows a perceptible increase in patenting in India and China but at different time points. Patents filing spiked in India soon after 2005 and in China

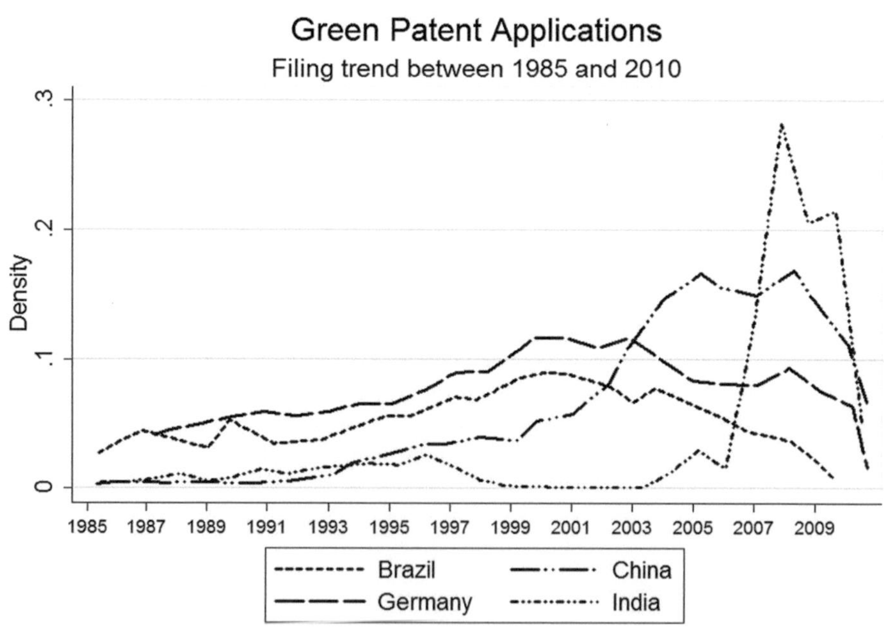

Fig. 6.1 Patent applications (1987–2010)

after 2001. In Brazil, there was a slow but steady increase in filings in the 1990s but it started to taper off around the year 2000. The argument that green technologies took the center stage of environmental technology in the past decade is not reflected in the filing trend in Germany, which witnessed a steady fall since 2003. In India, overall patenting activity was dormant until 2005 after which there was a huge spike in the applications filed from all types of applicants.

Patenting in China picked up roughly a decade earlier in the mid-1990s while Brazil witnessed sporadic spikes and dips in applications throughout the 1990s. Germany, on the contrary, saw a consistent rise in filings in the 1990s following by a steady fall in green patent filings after 2003. This was attributed to the increase in share of USA and Japan in "green" automotive technologies. Germany saw very little collaborative research between private companies and academic institutions getting reflected in joint filing of patents. Most of the private companies active in patenting "green" technologies in Germany are the big auto brands such as Robert Bosch GmbH.

It should be noted that the technologies being considered in this study are environment-friendly conventional technologies (such as a more fuel-efficient gasoline engine or a new filter for diesel exhaust emissions) and do not reflect non-conventional technologies such as improved fuel cells for cars or an enhanced electric vehicle. Therefore, apart from the impact of the financial crisis of 2007, the sharp decline in Germany can be attributed to the shift in focus to non-conventional automotive technologies. It was revealed in two interviews that the international combustion engine is here to stay till at least 2030 with major improvements in fuel use and emission reduction in conventional engines. The filing trend we see here suggests that companies may be gearing themselves up for the eventual technological shift in the future. Germany witnessed a sort of an "inverted-U" trend of patent filing in the past two decades with the peak coming around the year 2001 reflecting the beginning of the transition phase to non-conventional automotive technologies. The patent rush in China started in around the year 2000 with the surge in filings lasting till 2005. The picture is rather complicated in Brazil, which was doing well in terms of green innovations in the 1990s but, similar to Germany, witnessed a sharp fall since 2002.

An assignee list representing auto brands, identified in the data, is presented in the appendix. The top 5 applicants in 1990, 2000, 2005, and 2010 are also shown Figs. 6.2, 6.3, 6.4, and 6.5.

The total number of patent applications filed in different patent office is very different due to differences in the benchmark used to grant patents by the examiners and the difference in interpretation of the scope of each claim. Nevertheless, filing data allows us to decipher differences in preferences for technologies for which patents are applied. It also allows us to investigate the composition and behavior of assignees over time. Contrary to the industrial applicants, academic applicants

Fig. 6.2 Change in top 5 applicants in Germany over time

prefer to apply for "green" patents individually, with or without joint funding or joint research, with the slight exception of China.

This chapter presented a description of the patent data for Germany, India, China, and Brazil. An assessment of the composition of applicants and sources of priorities revealed significant differences across countries. Building on this, the next chapter will discuss the empirical methodology to determine the impact of stringency of environmental regulations on innovation and the results of the analyses. The following chapter will lay emphasis on the use of unweighted and weighted count of patent filings as measures of innovation to test the hypotheses that environmental regulation induces innovation in green transport technologies.

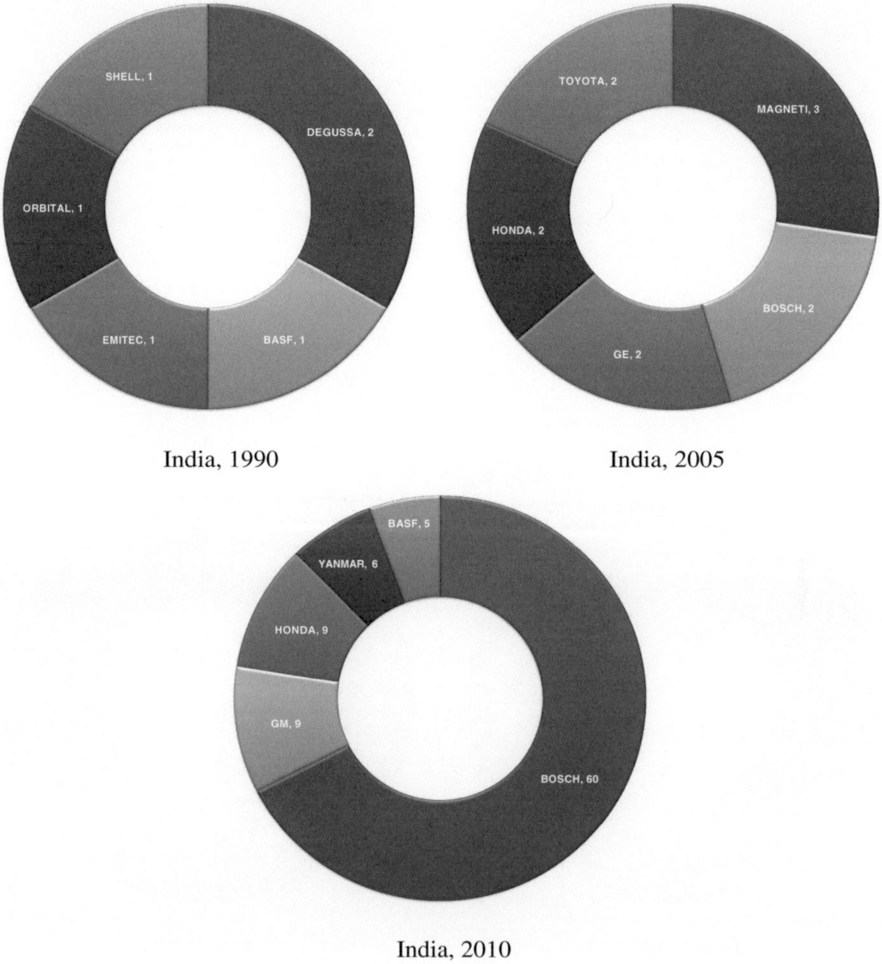

Fig. 6.3 Change in top 5 applicants in India (1990–2010)

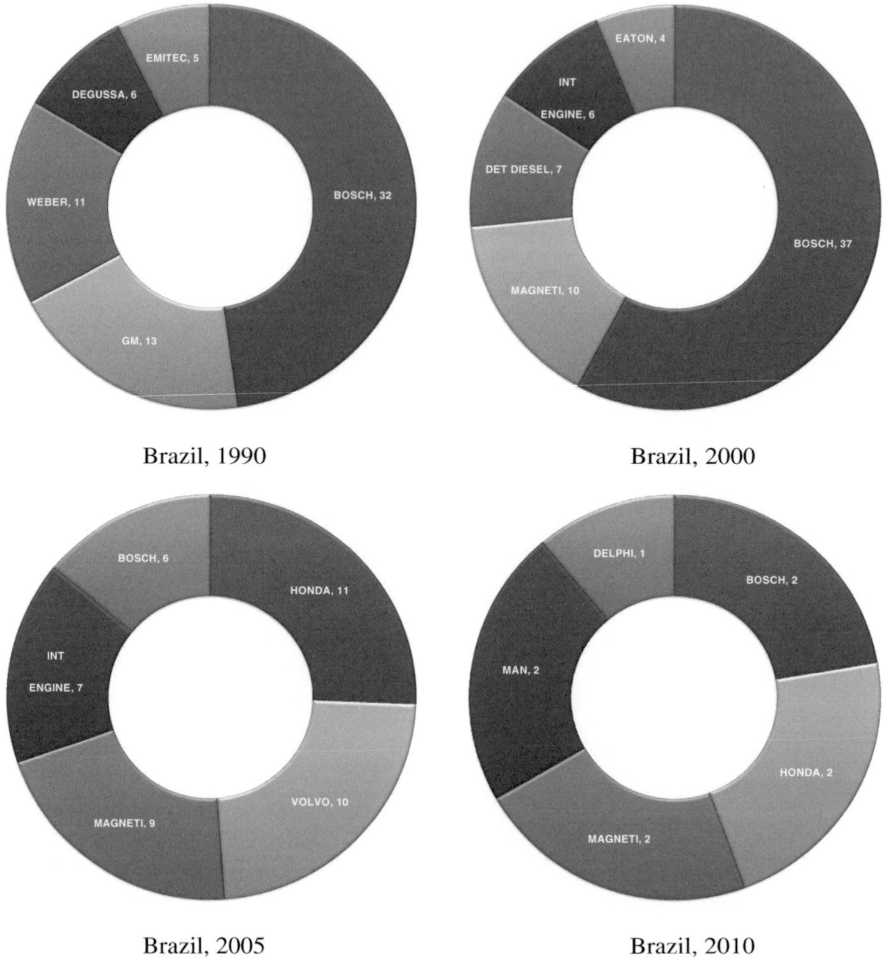

Fig. 6.4 Change in top 5 applicants in Brazil (1990–2010)

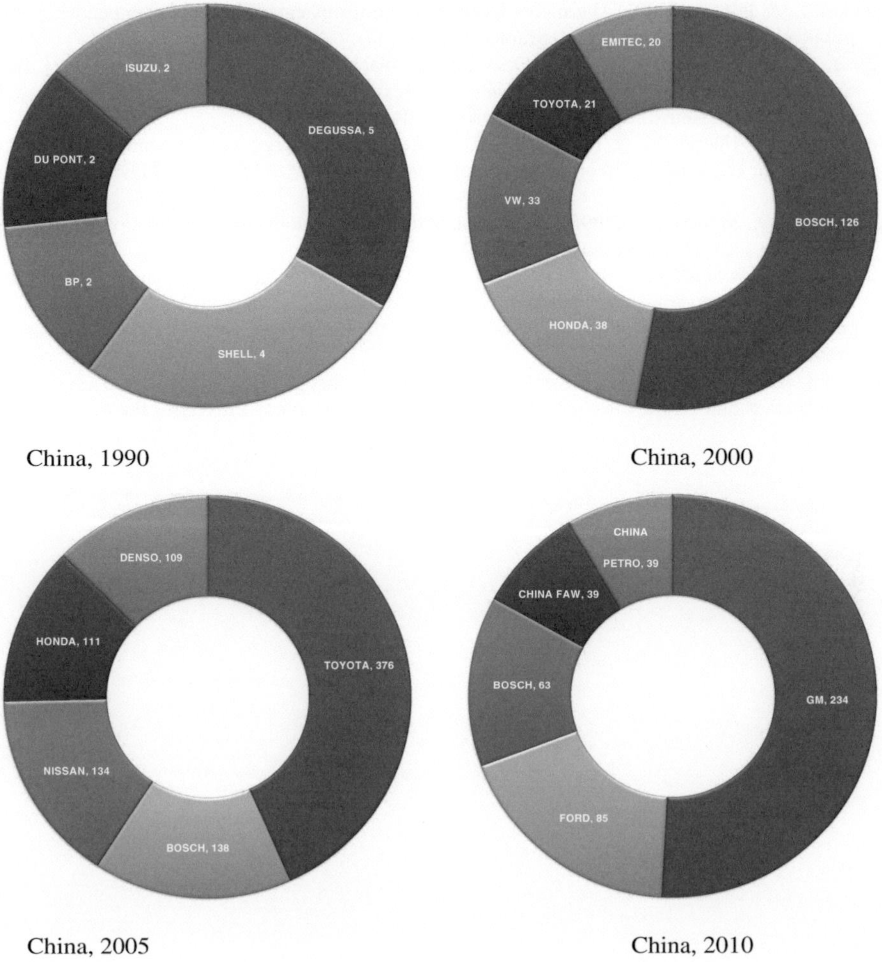

Fig. 6.5 Change in top 5 applicants in China (1990–2010)

References

Adams, R., J. Bessant, R. Phelps (2006) Innovation Management Measurement: A Review, *InternationalJournal of Management Reviews*, *8*(1), 21–47

Baker & McKenzie. (2012). Intellectual property: Patent trends around the world. Tower Club, Dallas, Texas: Intellectual Property Group.

Dechezleprêtre, A., Glachant, M., & Ménière, Y. (2010). What drives the international transfer of climate change mitigation technologies? Empirical evidence from patent data. FEEM Working Paper, Sustainable Development Series.

Griliches, Z. (1990). Patent statistics as economic indicators: A survey. *Journal of Economic Literature, 28*(4), 1661–1707.

Henkel, J., & Jell, F. (2009). Alternative motives to file for patents: Profiting from pendency and publication. TU Working Paper, Munich.

Hinze, S., & Schmoch, U. (2004). Opening the black box, In: Moed, H.F., Glänzel, W., Schmoch U. (eds.), *Handbook of quantitative science and technology studies*, 215–236 Dordrecht, The Netherlands: Kluwer Academic Publishers

Johnstone, N., Hascic, I., & Popp, D. (2010). Renewable energy policies and technological innovation: Evidence based on patent counts. *Environmental and Resource Economics, 45*(1), 133–155.

Lanjouw, J. O., & Mody, A. (1996). Innovation and the international diffusion of environmentally responsive technology. *Research Policy, 25*(4), 549–571.

Peters, C., & Pottelsberghe de la Potterie, B. (2006). Innovation strategy and the patenting behavior of firms. *Journal of Evolutionary Economics, 16*(1), 109–135.

Schmookler, J. (1966). Invention and economic growth. Cambridge, Mass.: Harvard University Press.

Schmookler, J. (1972). Patents, invention and economic change: Data and selected essays, ed. Z. Griliches and L. Hurwicz. Part II. Cambridge, Mass: Harvard University Press.

Chapter 7
Empirical Methodology and Findings

Abstract This chapter investigates the impact of the regulatory stringency index constructed in Chap. 5 on patenting in Germany, Brazil, India, and China from 1985 to 2010. The index is based on an aggregation of all relevant environmental regulations that were adopted in these countries since 1985. The index (core explanatory variable) is a good measure of strictness of environmental policies and regulations because it relies on all (incremental) interventions, i.e., vehicular emissions, fuel consumption level, and the technological developments to meet these requirements.

7.1 Introduction

In line with most existing empirical studies on innovation, this study uses patent applications as a proxy for innovation activity. All filings at the EPO and individual patent offices of Germany, India, Brazil, and China (selected by the "green" patent classes) were identified. Subsequently, those applications were selected that were registered in at least two offices, and only claimed priorities were chosen. Harhoff et al. (2003) and Guellec and de la Potterie (2000) have provided empirical justification for the use of this method wherein patent applications with a family size of more than one are considered.

Although priority date is a good approximation of the date of invention, the panel data in this study is sorted by application date. The reason why granted patents or existing patent portfolio could not be used was due to the fact that in India, China, and Brazil, being emerging economies, the general patenting activity picked up only in the last decade. Within this overall patenting, the share of "green" automotive patents was very low till 2002.

Patent pendency of at least 3 years in these countries led to insufficient data on granted patents for a longitudinal study. The descriptive statistics presented in Chap. 6 revealed that the rejection rate for patents applied between 1985 and 2010 was well below 7% in these countries signaling that most of the patents applied for in this area ended up being granted. Second, the patent data revealed that 25% of

A. Bharadwaj, *Environmental Regulations and Innovation in Advanced Automobile Technologies*, SpringerBriefs in Economics,
https://doi.org/10.1007/978-981-10-6952-9_7

Brazilian applications, 60% of Indian applications, and more than 20% of German applications till mid-2011 were not granted and were still under review at the time of data collection.

Although the share of granted German patents is high, using the low number in Brazil and India would have rendered an analysis meaningless. Using granted patents would have biased and led us to believe that the innovation activity in these countries is low or that it is being discouraged by regulatory changes. Hence, filing year, in the context of this study, is assumed to approximate innovation activity. Finally, it was revealed in interviews that the patents filed in most of the technology classes have originated outside India, China, and Brazil. Despite this fact, I was informed, several applicants in this industry are seeking patent protection before entering new markets in developing countries. Being wary of reverse engineering of new technologies, foreign companies are interested in reaping the first-mover advantage by giving competition to domestic players ("technological intimidation") through their patenting strategy.

7.2 Regulatory Stringency: Unweighted Patent Count

7.2.1 Principal Hypotheses and Model Specification

The research question being asked is whether the aggregate effect of regulatory stringency on overall patenting is positive or negative? This is being tested with the first hypothesis. The other question being asked is whether the effects of domestic and foreign regulatory stringency on domestic innovation at a disaggregated level are positive? In other words, what is the difference in effect of domestic versus foreign stringency on domestic innovation? The foreign regulation aspect of the latter questions pertains mainly to the developing countries, and they are being tested with the second and third hypotheses.

Hypothesis 1: On an aggregate level, "green" patenting increases as environmental regulations become more stringent.
Hypothesis 2: Patenting in "green" technologies in technologically proficient developing countries (TRDCs) increases as domestic environmental regulations become more stringent.
Hypothesis 3: Patenting in "green" technologies in technologically proficient developing countries (TRDCs) increases as foreign environmental regulations become more stringent.

Un-weighted count of all patent filings in the "green" technology classes between 1985 and 2010 and the share of these patent applications in total filings in the same period are used to test these first set of hypotheses. Annual un-weighted count of patents in $\log(\text{count}_{i,t}^{uw})$ is used as proxy for innovation. To test the above hypotheses, the following reduced-form equations are specified:

$$\text{count}^{uw}_{i,t} = \alpha + \beta_1 \text{rsi}_{i,t} + \beta_2 \text{gdp}_{i,t} + \beta_3 \text{totpat}_{i,t} + \delta_i \sum_{i=1}^{3} d_i + \epsilon_{\frac{i,t}{3}} \tag{7.1}$$

$$\text{count}^{uw}_{i,t} = \alpha + \beta_1 \text{rsi}_{i,t} + \beta_2 \text{gdp}_{i,t} + \beta_3 \text{totpat}_{i,t} + \delta\gamma_i \sum_{i=1}^{3} \text{rsi}_{i,t} d_i + \delta_i \sum_{i=1}^{3} d_i + \epsilon_{i,t} \tag{7.2}$$

where i = country and t = time (1986–2010). $\text{count}^{uw}_{i,t}$ is annual un-weighted count of patents (in logs). $\text{rsi}_{i,t}$ is the regulatory stringency index (in logs) constructed for all "green" patent classes, d_i are country dummies, $\text{gdp}_{i,t}$ is the gross domestic product in billion USD (in logs) at 2005 constant prices in year t and $\text{totpat}_{i,t}$ is the total number of patent applications received by the respective filing office, including direct and PCT national phase entries in year t and δ_i are country-level fixed effect.

7.2.2 Results

Tables 7.1 and 7.2 present preliminary results, but they do bring out statistically significant effect of regulatory stringency on patenting. These results show the disaggregate impact of regulations on patenting using a panel data of green patent filings in four countries for 25 years (1986–2010). The dependent variable is a simple annual un-weighted count of patents, and the independent variables are country-specific regulatory stringency index and country income. The dependent variable $\text{count}^{uw}_{\text{DE}}$ only signifies the presence of country-specific variables rsi_{DE} and gdp_{DE} in the specification. As expected, gdp in all countries has a positive and statistically significant effect on patenting.

Regulatory stringency only seems to have a statistically significant effect in Germany. The domestic effect is positive for Germany, India, and China, but it is negative for Brazil. To understand the impact of more stringent and older European regulations on patenting in non-European developing countries, cross-regulatory effects are investigated. They are presented in Table 7.2. With the same regression specification as above, it is found that rsi_{DE} has a statistically significant impact on patenting in all four countries. However, the effect is positive only in Germany, which suggests a strong positive domestic impact of regulation.

Innovation in developing countries is positively influenced by their domestic regulations, but the tightening of regulations in Germany seems to have a negative effect on innovation in all three economies. There are two reasons that can explain this. First, the fast emerging economies are inextricably linked with the European

Table 7.1 Disaggregated impact of regulatory stringency: OLS estimates 1

	(1) DE count^{uw}	(2) IN count^{uw}	(3) CN count^{uw}	(4) BR count^{uw}
log(rsi_{DE})	0.099***	0.003	0.001	−0.001
	(0.021)	(0.032)	(0.011)	(0.015)
log(rsi_{IN})		0.024		
		(0.081)		
log(gdp_{IN})		0.412***		
		(0.057)		
log(gdp_{DE})	0.898***			
	(0.014)			
log(rsi_{CN})			0.492***	
			(0.036)	
log(gdp_{CN})			0.639***	
			(0.019)	
log(rsi_{BR})				−0.004
				(0.056)
log(gdp_{BR})				0.713***
				(0.041)
Constant	−0.000	−0.015	−0.005	0.003
	(0.014)	(0.093)	(0.034)	(0.043)
N	96	96	96	96
R^2	0.999	0.771	0.993	0.979

Standard errors in parentheses ***$p < 0.01$, **$p < 0.05$, *$p < 0.1$
count^{uw} is the annual count un-weighted count of patents (in logs) for country; log(rsi_i) is the regulatory stringency index (in logs) constructed for all "green" patent classes for country i; log (gdp_i) is the gross domestic product in billion USD (in logs) at 2005 constant prices for country I; DE (Germany), IN (India), CN (China), and BR (Brazil)

and German economy. Any regulatory change here would certainly affect the economic and innovation climate (and subsequently the industrial sectors) in other countries. Second, the levels at which European regulations are presently too far-reaching ("excessively stringent") for some developing countries.[1] Any further push is likely to be perceived as a hindrance to innovation and growth.

The above regressions have a drawback of small number of observations due to the use of annual un-weighted count of patent applications in each country without taking into account differences across technology classes in which patents are filed. The problem of small sample size is addressed in the next section, which redefines the patent count variable by assigning IPC weights.

[1]The latter was pointed by an interviewee.

Table 7.2 Disaggregated impact of regulatory stringency: OLS estimates 2

	(1) DE log $count^{uw}$	(2) IN log $count^{uw}$	(3) CN log $count^{uw}$	(4) BR log $count^{uw}$
$\log(rsi_{DE})$	1.307***	−0.149***	−0.287***	−0.104***
	(0.05)	(0.05)	(0.05)	(0.04)
$\log(rsi_{IN})$	−0.157***	0.421***	−0.316***	−0.115***
	(0.06)	(0.06)	(0.06)	(0.05)
$\log(rsi_{CN})$	−0.188***	−0.196***	1.312***	−0.138***
	(0.07)	(0.07)	(0.07)	(0.06)
$\log(rsi_{BR})$	−0.152***	−0.158***	−0.305***	0.851***
	(0.05)	(0.06)	(0.05)	(0.04)
Constant	0.75***	0.78***	1.50***	0.546***
	(0.22)	(0.22)	(0.21)	(0.17)
N	96	96	96	96
R^2	0.94	0.67	0.93	0.91

Standard errors in parentheses ***$p < 0.01$, **$p < 0.05$, *$p < 0.1$
$\log(count^{uw})$ is the annual un-weighted count of patents (in logs) for country i; $\log(rsi_i)$ is the regulatory stringency index (in logs) constructed for all "green" patent classes for country i. DE (Germany), IN (India), CN (China), and BR (Brazil)

7.3 Regulatory Stringency: Weighted Patent Count

7.3.1 Principal Hypotheses

The Porter hypothesis talks about a sort of trigger effect of an environmental regulation on innovation. While the argument is based on a normative relationship between regulation and innovation, it does not show innovation actually taking place eventually. The concept of induced innovation is, therefore, broader than what Porter suggested in the sense that the end result is a measurable increase in innovation activity as a result of the regulation.

This section presents the results of regulatory stringency on patenting at an aggregate level and at country levels. The results presented here are from the full sample of all technology classes assigned in the patent applications. The results are later replicated for a subsample of selected "green" technology classes. There could still be a potential bias emanating from an omitted variable. Controlling for country-specific fixed effects and technology class-specific fixed effect solves this problem.

Time fixed effects at an aggregate country level help resolve the potential bias, which could arise from any country-specific effect that is correlated with both patenting and regulatory stringency. Descriptive statistics of variables used in this analysis are presented in Table 7.1. Based on this, the following hypotheses are formulated which are replicated from the previous section. The first hypothesis being tested is whether the aggregate effect of regulatory stringency on overall patenting is positive or negative. The second and third hypotheses test the positive effect of domestic and foreign regulatory stringency on domestic innovation at a disaggregated level.

Hypothesis 1: On an aggregate level, "green" patenting, relative to patenting in other areas, increases as environmental regulations become stringent.
Hypothesis 2: Patenting in "green" technologies, relative to "non-green" technologies, in technologically proficient developing countries (TRDCs) increases as domestic environmental regulations become more stringent.
Hypothesis 3: Patenting in "green" technologies, relative to "non-green" technologies, in technologically proficient developing countries (TRDCs) increases as foreign environmental regulations become more stringent.

The innovation measure used in this section is motivated by the work of Trajtenberg (1990) in which a count of patents was created using a number of citations as weights. Tratjtenberg's study showed that a weighted count of patents is a better measure of innovation in certain technological areas than an un-weighted count. The measure used in this study relies on a weighing design, where only those IPCs, which, for the purpose of this study, are classified as "green" are considered. This design is based on the argument that several patents applied in the automotive domain are not "green," i.e., they are neither emission reducing nor fuel saving. Hence, this selective weighting design ensures that all irrelevant patents have no bearing on the weighted count.

Based on Shane and Klocks' (1997) weighted patent citation measure, this study also follows a linear weighting scheme. Let ipc_n be the total number of patent classes assigned in patent n in its filing in year t and let N be the total number of patent filings in year t such that $\text{count}_t = \sum_n^N \text{ipc}_n$.

To test the above hypotheses, the following reduced-form equation is specified:

$$\text{count}^w_{i,k,t} = \alpha + \beta_1 \text{rsi}_{i,k,t} + \beta_{2\text{gdp}_{i,k,t}} + \delta_i \sum_{i=1}^{3} d_i + \lambda_k \sum_{k=1}^{22} d_i + \tau_k \sum_{t=1}^{23} d_t + \epsilon_{i,k,t} \quad (7.3)$$

where i = country, k = technology − class, and t = time (1986–2010). $\text{count}^w_{i,k,t}$ is annual weighted count of patents (in logs), $\text{rsi}_{i,k,t}$ is the regulatory stringency index (in logs) constructed for all green patent classes, d_i are country dummies, λ_k are class dummies, and τ_t are time dummies. $\epsilon_{i,k,t}$ captures the residual variation. Additional explanatory variables are considered in the next count data model specification.

There were very few counts of patents registered in the 1980s, particularly in India, China, and Brazil. Therefore, the sample had to be restricted, starting from 1985. Since the data for the year 2011 was not complete for India and Brazil at the time of compilation, it had to be dropped. There was missing information for Brazil in years 1985 and 1986. Finally, the sample was restricted to 24 years, from 1987 to 2010. In the full sample, there were 23 recorded technology classes comprising of

Table 7.3 Descriptive statistics: full sample

Variable	Obs	Mean	Std. dev.	Min	Max
count	2208	57.05	159.42	0	1488
share	2185	0.001	0.002	0	0.030
rsi	2208	5.45	13.15	0	91
gdp	2208	1377.49	943.12	283.63	3880.00
totpat	2185	44676.25	65843.16	3424	391,177

"green" and "non-green" IPCs. Patent applications considered in the sample have at least one "green" technology class assigned to them. In total, this yielded a data set of 2208 observations in the full sample comprising four countries, twenty-three patent classes, and twenty-four years; and 576 observations in the subsample comprising four countries, six patent classes, and twenty-four years.

The problems in transforming variables with zeroes into logarithm are solved by taking log(1 + count) instead. In some cases, the regulatory stringency is introduced with a lag. This served two purposes—first, it takes into account the "announcement effect" of a regulatory intervention by the industry, and second, it deals with reverse causality which can be a potential problem between regulation and innovation activity. Explanatory variables, including the regulatory stringency index variable, are used with a time lag of 1, 3, and 5 years.[2] Fixed effects (country-specific) are used to control unobserved heterogeneity. Table 7.3 provides a summary of the descriptive statistics.

7.3.2 Preliminary Results

This section discusses preliminary results of OLS fixed effects estimations using a weighted patent filing as the dependent variable. Since the observations are not independent, heteroskedasticity robust standard errors are clustered at the class-country level (clustered sandwich estimator) and are reported in parentheses.[3] On an aggregate level, *rsi* has a positive and statistically significant effect on the weighted count of patents. The individual country effects are negative and vary slightly across the countries considered. But what we see here can be misleading because the *rsi* variable here is a composite (cumulative) regulatory stringency index for all green technology classes and not and not country-specific indices. The weighted count of patents are overall counts and not country specifics, and other

[2]The choice of lag lengths was based on interviews where I was told about the approximate time the industry expects the government to inform them, prior to announcing any new regulation.

[3]In this regression framework, the panel variable is a unique country (4)–ipc (23) id which makes the total panel groups 92. The time variable has 24 years with year 2011 dropped because of missing information. The total observations are therefore 2208.

regressions merely show the aggregate effects of stringency on overall patenting. Country dummies are used to tease out country-level effects, and technology effects are considered but these results may not be showing the most accurate picture. This leads us to an alternative model specification, which takes into account the peculiarities of this patent data.

7.3.3 Alternate Model Specification

Since the number of patent applications is essentially a count of non-negative integers, resorting to another distribution, such as negative binomial or Poisson, would be a more plausible choice even though they impose strict constraints on the count probability which will be based only on the expected counts. Compared to Poisson model, the negative binomial model allows the variance and conditional mean of the count dependent variable to be different. There is another advantage of using negative binomial over Poisson model. In the former, a (pseudo)-ML approach can be used to estimate robust coefficients even under a mis-specified underlying distribution function. Therefore, count data technique is used as the next empirical strategy and equation is estimated using a negative binomial model (Table 7.4).[4]

Here, the event counts are the weighted count of patent filings received at the EPO, Indian Patent Office, Brazilian Patent Office, and the Chinese Patent Office. A count of an occurring event is simply the realization of a random integer value, which is strictly non-negative. Formally, in the fixed effects Poisson model for regression in panel data, the dependent variable $\text{count}_{i,t}$ varies across panel entity i and over time t and follows a Poisson distribution with parameter $\mu_{i,t}$. This parameter is determined by a vector of exogenous variables $x_{i,t}$ which follows a log-lin function such that $\ln \mu_{i,t} = \delta_i + \beta x_{i,t}$ where δ_i control country-specific fixed effects. The conventional maximum likelihood (ML) Poisson regression includes $n - 1$ individual dummy variables to estimate δ fixed effects. Alternatively, the ML method can be conditional on the sum such that $\sum_t \text{count}_{i,t} \forall i$.

According to Cameron and Trivedi (1998), both methods of Poisson estimation yield the exact same estimates for β and the covariance matrix and the final choice of method is determined by convenience of computation (Allison and Waterman 2002). Although the Poisson models with fixed effects will allow forth severe heterogeneity across the countries being considered, they do not allow forum restricted intra-country heterogeneity.

This is because it imposes the restrictive assumption that the mean count in each country or each technology class is the same as the variance, i.e., $E(\text{count}_{i,t}) = var(\text{count}_{i,t}) = \mu_{i,t}$. This is an assumption that is unlikely to be met in most data,

[4]For details on count models, see Cameron and Trivedi (1998), Hausman et al. (1984), and Maddala (1983); for a comparative assessment see Allison and Waterman (2002).

Table 7.4 Aggregate impact of regulatory stringency

	(1) log count^w	(2) log count^w	(3) log count^w	(4) log count^w
log(rsi)	0.255***	0.260***	0.286***	0.264***
	(0.075)	(0.077)	(0.072)	(0.078)
log(GDP)	0.887***	1.957***	0.794***	1.898***
	(0.117)	(0.162)	(0.128)	(0.215)
D_{IN}			−2.171***	−0.516
			(0.327)	(0.410)
D_{CN}			−0.343	0.417*
			(0.367)	(0.252)
D_{BR}			−1.178***	0.158
			(0.343)	(0.344)
Constant	−4.224***	−14.000***	−2.667***	−13.566***
	(0.772)	(1.246)	(1.012)	(1.905)
Year effects	No	Yes	No	Yes
Class effects	No	Yes	No	Yes
N	2,208	2,208	2,208	2,208
R^2	0.545	0.783	0.603	0.811
χ^2	94.6	1399.6	330.6	2518.7
Prob. > χ^2	0.00	0.00	0.00	0.00

Robust standard errors in parentheses ***$p < 0.01$, **$p < 0.05$, *$p < 0.1$
log(count^w) is the annual weighted count of patents (in logs); log(rsi) is the regulatory stringency index (in logs); log(gdp) is the gross domestic product in billion USD (in logs) at 2005 constant prices; D_i are country dummies for India (IN), China (CN), and Brazil (BR) with dummy for Germany as the intercept

particularly in patent data. Therefore, the model is more suitable to a negative binomial general specification than to a Poisson model because the former allows each individual panel entity to have its own individual Poisson parameter. Here, the weighted patent count variables $\text{count}^w_{i,t}$ follow a negative binomial distribution which is essentially a generalization of the Poisson distribution with an extra parameter included to allow heterogeneity in the variance to exceed the mean. Hausman, Hall, and Griliches (1984) used one of the many ways to parameterize the NB distribution, where the conditional parameter (λ) is determined by the covariates such that the mass of the NB function

$$f(\text{count}_{i,t}|\lambda_{i,t}, \theta_i) = \frac{\Gamma(\lambda_{i,t} + \text{count}_{i,t})}{\Gamma(\lambda_{i,t})\Gamma(\text{count}_{i,t} + 1)} \left(\frac{\theta_i}{1+\theta_i}\right)^{\text{count}_{i,t}} \left(\frac{1}{1+\theta_i}\right)^{\lambda_{i,t}} \tag{7.4}$$

where θ_i does not vary over time for individual entity i, $\ln\ \lambda_{i,t} = \beta x_{i,t}$ with the mean $E(\text{count}_{i,t}) = \theta_i \lambda_{i,t}$ and the variance $\text{Var}(\text{count}_{i,t}) = (1+\theta_i)\theta_i\lambda_{i,t}$ since $\frac{E(\text{count}_{i,t})}{\text{Var}(\text{count}_{i,t})} = 1 + \theta_i,$ variation is allowed across individuals but not over time.

Further, it is assumed that for each i, over time, the $\text{count}_{i,t}$ are independent which implies that $\sum_t \text{count}_{i,t}$ also follow an NB distribution $(\theta_i, \sum_i \lambda_{i,t})$.

7.3.4 Results

The estimates of the reduced-form model of weighted count of "green" patent using a panel of Germany, India, China, and Brazil over the period 1987–2010 are reported in Table 7.5.[5] Taking the fixed country effects into account, the regulatory stringency is always positive and significant whether time fixed effects and technology-specific FEs are included or not. The reference country dummy category of Germany has a large negative (and significant) sign relative to the smaller positive dummies of other three countries.

It is interesting to see the differences in effects of regulatory stringency on patenting across countries. In order to achieve this, regulation variable *rsi* was interacted with country dummies D_i. These results are presented in estimations (3) and (4) in Table 7.5. With the exception of India, regulatory stringency in all other countries has a positive (and significant) effect on aggregate patenting.

After investigating the role of regulatory stringency of overall patenting in automotive technologies, the following section shifts focus to the subsample of selected green technology classes discussed at length in Chap. 5. The above estimation results are replicated for this smaller sample of six key technology classes over the same time period of 24 years and four countries. These estimations control for year effects and technology-/IPC-specific effects (called "class effects"). Lagged regulatory stringency is also used to account for a potential announcement effect of the regulatory change in the industry for the latter to brace itself, technologically and financially.

$$\begin{aligned} \text{rsi}_{k,c,t} &= \text{rsi index} \quad \text{if } k \in (1, .., 6)\text{green IPC classes} \\ &= 0 \quad \text{otherwise} \end{aligned}$$

where $\text{rsi}_{k,c,t}$ is the regulatory stringency index specifically for the green regulated technology classes (k) under the IPC system calculated for time period t = 1987–2010.

Descriptive statistics of the variables used in the examination of the subsample of core "green" technologies are presented in Table 7.6. The average count of filing of a "green" patent application is 186 with a large standard deviation of 264 due to the differences in the four countries that are included in the study. The focus of patenting in the three emerging countries (BIC) was initially weak, which explains a large number of zeros encountered in the weighted patent counts during the 1980s

[5]The estimates are derived using Huber–White standard errors to control for heteroskedasticity for a shorter time period. Years 1985, 1986, and 2011 had to be dropped due to inconsistency.

Table 7.5 Estimates Based on a Negative Binomial Model

	(1) $count^w$	(2) $count^w$	(3) $count^w$	(4) $count^w$
log(rsi)	0.255***	0.251***		
	(0.03)	(0.023)		
log(GDP)	2.178***	0.723***		
	(0.071)	(0.043)		
D_{IN}	−0.245	−1.107***		
	(0.181)	(0.172)		
D_{CN}	1.242***	0.287***		
	(0.12)	(0.106)		
D_{BR}	2.140***	0.459***		
	(0.175)	(0.118)		
log(rsi_{DE})			0.011***	0.013***
			(0.003)	(0.002)
log(rsi_{IN})			−0.055***	−0.012***
			(0.007)	(0.006)
log(rsi_{CN})			0.086***	0.071***
			(0.004)	(0.004)
log(rsi_{BR})			0.009***	0.011***
			(0.004)	(0.003
Constant	−19.03***	−5.10***	−0.74***	0.13***
	(0.66)	(0.35)	(0.25)	(0.04)
Year effects	Yes	No	Yes	No
Class effects	Yes	No	Yes	No
N	2,208	2,208	2,208	2,208
(log) likelihood	−6650.3	−7148.1	−7110.2	−7358.6
χ^2	2561.8	753.1	1141.1	454.2
Prob. > χ^2	0.00	0.00	0.00	0.00

Robust standard errors in parentheses ***$p < 0.01$, **$p < 0.05$, *$p < 0.1$
$count^w$ is the annual weighted count of patents; log(rsi) is the regulatory stringency index (in logs) constructed for all green patent classes for country *i*; log(gdp) is the gross domestic product in billion USD (in logs) at 2005 constant prices; D_i are country dummies for India (IN), China (CN), and Brazil (BR) with dummy for Germany as the intercept

Table 7.6 Descriptive statistics: sub-sample

Variable	Obs	Mean	Std. dev.	Min	Max
count	594	186.5	264.2	0	1488
rsi	600	24.4	27.0	0	195
patindex	600	3.7	1.0	2.0	5.0
gdp	600	1419.7	981.6	283.6	4236.9
totcar	558	2,158,782	2,445,342	57,678	14,488,100
totpat	594	49501.9	80591.5	3424	526,412
gas	528	571886.4	347,691	83000	1,754,000

Table 7.7 Correlation matrix

	count	rsi	patnidex	gdp	totcar	totpat	gas
count	1.00						
rsi	0.21	1.00					
patindex	0.56	0.30	1.00				
gdp	0.57	0.26	0.88	1.00			
totcar	0.36	0.14	0.62	0.83	1.00		
totpat	0.30	0.05	0.51	0.71	0.91	1.00	
gas	0.29	−0.11	0.62	0.69	0.77	0.83	1.00

and 1990s. The statistical range of *rsi* is also high depicting the end points and the potential of tightening environmental regulations over time. Further, the direction of change in strictness of environmental regulations is always positive [d(rsi)/d(*t*) > 0]. Table 7.7 shows the correlation matrix of variables used in the analysis, which determined the choice of independent variables. As before, log($count^w$) is the annual weighted count of patents (in logs) for country *i*; log(rsi_i) is the regulatory stringency index (in logs) constructed for all "green" patent classes for country *i*; log(gdp_i) is the gross domestic product in billion USD (in logs) at 2005 constant prices for country *i*; D_i are country dummies for India (IN), China (CN), and Brazil (BR) with dummy for Germany as the intercept; *patindex* is index of strictness of IPR regime which was calculated based on Park's (2008) methodology; *totcar* is number of all new registrations of passenger cars, both petrol and diesel and all engine sizes; *totgas* is the consumption of gasoline for road transport (in logs) in barrels per day. As expected, there is high positive correlation of *gdp* with *patentindex* and *totcar*. Tables 7.8 and 7.9 report OLS and negative binomial estimates with a panel of four countries, six technology classes, and 24 years.

While stringency of environmental regulations in India and China positively affects patenting, it is the opposite in the case of Brazil. With the exception of Brazil, effects of *RSI* in Germany, India, and China are positive if there is a lag of 3–5 years. These are important results, which were corroborated by the German interviewees. Controlling for technology-specific effects did not have an impact on the findings.

The strength of patent system measured by the *patindex* variable is consistently significant and positive which means that the patenting activity across the four countries increases with strictness of the IPR regime. *totcar* is significant and positive implying that an increase in car sales boosts induces firms to bring new technologies into these countries.

Table 7.8 Panel Data Estimates: sub-sample

	(1) log(count^w)	(2) log(count^w)	(3) log(count^w)	(4) log(count^w)
log(rsi$_{DE}$)	−0.001	−0.000		
	(0.004)	(0.004)		
log(rsi$_{IN}$)	0.007**	0.007**		
	(0.003)	(0.003)		
log(rsi$_{CN}$)	0.017	0.016		
	(0.011)	(0.010)		
log(rsi$_{BR}$)	−0.064***	−0.063***		
	(0.008)	(0.007)		
log(patindex)	3.212***	3.213***	1.766***	1.767***
	(0.238)	(0.235)	(0.375)	(0.377)
log(gdp)	−0.408	−0.509	−0.498	−0.508
	(0.341)	(0.323)	(0.440)	(0.438)
log(totcar)	0.265*	0.307**	0.416**	0.418**
	(0.141)	(0.137)	(0.181)	(0.181)
log(rsi)			0.187**	0.190**
			(0.077)	(0.078)
D_{IN}			0.212	0.203
			(0.498)	(0.445)
D_{CN}			0.082	0.084
			(0.619)	(0.256)
D_{BR}			−1.860***	−1.870***
			(0.633)	(0.314)
Constant	−0.304	−1.641	−0.350	−1.688*
	(1.270)	(1.298)	(1.070)	(0.929)
Class effects	No	Yes	No	Yes
Observations	524	524	518	518
R^2	0.504	0.729	0.514	0.725
χ^2	425.3	600.6	143.2	1366.3
Prob. > χ^2	0.00	0.00	0.00	0.00

Standard errors in parentheses ***$p < 0.01$, **$p < 0.05$, *$p < 0.1$

log(count^w) is the annual weighted count of patents (in logs) for country; log(rsi$_i$) is the regulatory stringency index (in logs) constructed for all "green" patent classes for country *i*; log(gdp$_i$) is the gross domestic product in billion USD (in logs) at 2005 constant prices for country *i*; D_i are country dummies for India (IN), China (CN), and Brazil (BR) with dummy for Germany as the intercept; *patindex* is the index of strictness of IPR regime based on methodology proposed by Park (2008); *totcar* is the number of all new registrations of passenger cars, both petrol and diesel and all engine sizes; *totgas* is the consumption of gasoline for road transport (in logs) in barrels per day

Table 7.9 Negative Binomial Model: sub-sample panel data

	(1) log ($count^w$)	(2) log ($count^w$)	(3) log ($count^w$)	(4) log ($count^w$)	(5) log ($count^w$)
rsi_{DE}	−0.004	−0.018			
	(0.004)	(0.004)			
rsi_{IN}	0.012***	0.005***			
	(0.001)	(0.001)			
rsi_{CN}	0.023***	0.004			
	(0.005)	(0.005)			
rsi_{BR}	−0.011**	−0.034***			
	(0.006)	(0.005)			
log(patindex)	0.610**	0.603**	0.649**	1.097***	0.986***
	(0.277)	(0.257)	(0.263)	(0.271)	−(0.304)
log(gdp)	0.323	0.382**	0.274	0.043	0.31
	(0.202)	(0.188)	(0.19)	(0.20)	(0.19)
log(totcar)	0.349***	0.260***	0.336***	0.565**	0.441***
	(0.072)	(0.067)	(0.076)	(0.08)	(0.064)
$L1(rsi_{DE})$			−0.015***		
			(0.005)		
$L3(rsi_{DE})$				0.006**	
				(0.003)	
$L5(rsi_{DE})$					0.004*
					(0.002)
$L1(rsi_{CN})$			0.002		
			(0.005)		
$L3(rsi_{CN})$				0.008	
				(0.007)	
$L5(rsi_{CN})$					0.027***
					(0.007)
$L1(rsi_{BR})$			−0.033***		
			(0.007)		
$L3(rsi_{BR})$				−0.019***	
				(0.005)	
$L5(rsi_{BR})$					−0.003
					(0.005)
Constant	−7.246***	−5.581***	−6.150***	−9.429***	−9.639***
	(0.997)	(1.11)	(1.41)	(0.786)	(0.758)
Year effects	Yes	Yes	Yes	Yes	Yes
Class effects	No	Yes	Yes	Yes	Yes

(continued)

Table 7.9 (continued)

	(1) log ($count^w$)	(2) log ($count^w$)	(3) log ($count^w$)	(4) log ($count^w$)	(5) log ($count^w$)
Observations	552	552	551	549	557
Log (likelihood)	−2773.8	−2736.0	−2749.5	−2744.8	−2741.0
χ^2	1312.1	1744.9	1535.8	1523.6	1471.7
Prob. > χ^2	0.00	0.00	0.00	0.00	0.00

Robust standard errors in parentheses ***$p < 0.01$, **$p < 0.05$, *$p < 0.1$
*L*1, *L*3, *L*5 are lagged index values (in logs) of 1, 3, 5 years to capture announcement effect of regulatory change

7.4 Standard Difference-In-Difference Analysis

7.4.1 Model Specification

This section deals with the analysis of two specific regulations in each of the four countries using a standard difference-in-difference (DID) method. In estimating the DID estimator in a regression framework, it is easy to calculate the standard errors while controlling for any other variable which may reduce the residual variance. Two groups were identified from the full sample:

- Weighted patent filings in the "non-green" category as the control group
- Weighted patent filings in the "green" category as the treatment group.

Total patenting in each country for that technology is taken as an additional covariate in the analysis. The first time point considered is the year 2000 in which Germany adopted the Euro III emission norms, India adopted the Euro II equivalent (Bharat Stage II) norms, China adopted the Euro I equivalent (China 1) norms, and Brazil implemented the Euro II equivalent (PROCONVE *L*3 and *P*4) norms.

Given the differences in strictness of the adopted regulations, DID estimates are provided for each country separately. The second time point considered is the year 2005 in which Germany adopted the Euro IV emission norms, India adopted the Euro III equivalent (Bharat Stage III) norms, China adopted the Euro III equivalent (China 3) norms, and Brazil also implemented the Euro III equivalent (PROCONVE *L*4 and *P*5) norms.

$$\text{post}_{t00} = \begin{cases} 1, & \text{if } t \geq \text{year 2000} \\ 0 & \text{if } t < \text{year 2000} \end{cases} \quad \text{and} \quad \text{post}_{t05} = \begin{cases} 1, & \text{if } t \geq \text{year 2005} \\ 0 & \text{if } t < \text{year 2005} \end{cases}$$

Given the difference in strictness of the adopted regulations, DID estimates are provided for each country separately. We have a repeated cross section of patent filings in 23 technology areas for 24 years for a country.

$$\text{count}^{w}_{i,k,t} = \alpha + \beta_1 \text{post}_{t*} + \beta_2 \text{treatment} + \beta_3 \text{interaction} + \beta_4 \text{totpak}_{i.k.t} + u_{i,k,t} \quad (7.5)$$

where $\text{count}^{w}_{i,k,t}$ is the annual weighted count of patents (in logs) for country i in technology class k in time t; log(totpat) is the total number of patent applications (in logs) in that technology received in a year by the respective filing office, including direct and PCT national phase entries; post_{t*} is a dummy which is 1 for time period from the implementation of the regulation in year t and zero otherwise; *treatment* is a dummy which is 1 for all "green" technology classes and zero otherwise; *interaction* is the interaction dummy of post_{00} and *treatment*. All residual errors are captured by $u_{i,k,t}$.

7.4.2 Results

The major differences in the impact of the regulatory intervention in the year 2005 (Table 7.11) are seen only in the emerging economies of China, India, and Brazil. In this case patenting in the control category declined in China, regulation negatively (though statistically insignificant) affects "green" patenting, and India witnesses a sizable increase in "green" patenting after the implementation of the more stringent regulation in 2005.

The variable *treatment* captures the possible differences between the two groups prior to the regulatory intervention. The time dummy *post* captures the aggregate factors that can cause variation in patent filing despite the regulation. Finally, the most important variable for this analysis is the interaction term, which will capture the difference in difference, i.e., β_3 will capture the difference between (a) and (b), where (a) is the pre- and postdifference in "green" filings and (b) is the pre- and postdifference in "non-green" filings.

These results are presented in Tables 7.10 and 7.11.

The results for the year 2000 show that there is a significant positive effect of *treatment* in Germany, China, and Brazil. This means that, except in India, there was an initial difference between the two groups in all countries and that patenting in "green" technologies outweighed patenting in "non-green" technologies with the difference being highest in Germany. Coefficient for post_{00} is significant in all and is only negative in China.

This implies that only China witnessed an increase in "non-green" filing, which is being driven by the significant effect of overall patenting. The coefficient of the core variable *interaction* is significant and positive in all except in Brazil. This means that the regulation did play a role in the increase in "green" patent filing due to the implementation of Euro III in Germany and Euro II equivalent in India and Euro I equivalent norms in China.

Table 7.10 Difference-in-difference estimation: year 2000

	$\log\left(\text{count}^w_{\text{DE}}\right)$	$\log\left(\text{count}^w_{\text{IN}}\right)$	$\log\left(\text{count}^w_{\text{CN}}\right)$	$\log\left(\text{count}^w_{\text{BR}}\right)$
post_{00}	−0.921***	−4.886***	0.519***	−0.415***
	(0.122)	(1.142)	(0.161)	(0.130)
treatment	2.001***	1.849	1.446***	1.759***
	(0.470)	(1.285)	0.364	(0.274)
interaction	0.440***	9.751***	1.203***	0.144
	(0.158)	(1.335)	(0.177)	(0.157)
log(totpat)	1.764***	3.274***	0.195***	0.372***
	(0.325)	(0.612)	(0.617)	(0.121)
Constant	−15.554***	−27.662***	−0.009	−2.219**
	(3.497)	(5.245)	(0.640)	(1.120)
Observations	545	575	490	437
R^2	0.35	0.24	0.48	0.38
χ^2	79.36	135.2	345.9	58.1
Prob. > χ^2	0.00	0.00	0.00	0.00

Table 7.11 Difference-in-difference estimation: year 2005

	$\log\left(\text{count}^w_{\text{DE}}\right)$	$\log\left(\text{count}^w_{\text{IN}}\right)$	$\log\left(\text{count}^w_{\text{CN}}\right)$	$\log\left(\text{count}^w_{\text{BR}}\right)$
post_{05}	−1.291***	−0.394	−1.450***	−1.190***
	(0.099)	(1.202)	(0.153)	(0.113)
treatment	2.109***	1.561	1.725***	1.897***
	(0.457)	(1.176)	(0.346)	(0.248)
interaction	0.477***	17.748***	1.220***	−0.054
	(0.161)	(1.350)	(0.186)	(0.162)
log(totpat)	1.412***	0.328	0.833***	0.668***
	(0.212)	(0.581)	(0.054)	(0.079)
Constant	−11.849***	−2.746	−6.337***	−4.964***
	(2.306)	(5.119)	(0.598)	(0.750)
Observations	545	575	490	437
R^2	0.38	0.36	0.49	0.45
χ^2	208.7	272.7	388.4	212.1
Prob. > χ^2	0.00	0.00	0.00	0.00

Standard errors in parentheses ***$p < 0.01$, **$p < 0.05$, *$p < 0.1$

log(count^w) is the annual weighted count of patents (in logs) for country *i*; log(totpat) is the total number of patent applications (in logs) received in a year by the respective filing office, including direct and PCT national phase entries; post 0*t* is a dummy which is 1 for time period from the implementation of the regulation in year *t* and zero otherwise; *treatment* is a dummy which is 1 for all "green" technology classes and zero otherwise; *interaction* is the interaction dummy of post_{00} and *treatment*

7.5 Findings

The results presented in this study provide preliminary evidence of an inducement effect of regulatory stringency to innovation activity as measured by weighted patent counts. The hypothesis that domestic stringency positively affects innovation in developing countries is not rejected. This gives support to the Porter hypothesis that well-crafted government regulations can lead to more innovation. A reliable and stricter intellectual property regime is more likely to induce such innovation activity. This is a rather straightforward finding in the sense that foreign and domestic companies get assurance from a IP regime, where their rights are enforceable and generally, the legal environment for innovations is more secure. Car sales were found positively correlated.

This is especially true in the emerging economies, where the market is not yet saturated and vehicles are still not necessities for people. Car companies invest a lot in lucrative offers and campaigns to lure the first timers, and, in light of this, car sales are taken to be a big incentive for companies to raise the innovation bar higher.

With the exception of Brazil, the announcement effects played a crucial role. In the context of the technologically proficient countries considered in the study, this could be due to three possible factors.

First, advanced technologies are mostly sourced from innovative companies in industrialized countries such as Germany. Further, the same companies are attracted by the immense economic potential of these markets for their businesses. To be able to sell their advanced technologies, whether embodied in vehicles or directly to other manufacturers, procuring companies in the host countries need to create products compatible with these technologies. This acts as an incentive for the host country to try to match their environmental standards with that of the industrialized country.

Second, foreign technological partnerships by companies in the developing world are a source of better technology, resources, markets, and opportunities. Having a level playing field in terms of environmental standards and policies is a precursor to forge such fruitful collaborations.

Third, countries such as China and India are increasingly bearing the brunt in climate change negotiations and talks. This is due to the sustained increase in their share of global emissions when the rest of the world is investing in bringing the emissions down.

Managerial and public policy implications in the overall context of the study are discussed in Chap. 8.

References

Allison, P. D., & Waterman, R. P. (2002). Fixed effects negative binomial regression models. *Sociological Methodology, 32,* 247–265.

Cameron, A. C., & Trivedi, P. K. (1998). *Regression analysis of count data*. Cambridge, NY: Cambridge University Press.

Guellec, D., & de la Potterie, B. V. P. (2000). Applications, grants and the value of a patent. *Economics Letters, 69,* 109–114.

Harhoff, D., Scherer, F. M., & Vopel, K. (2003). Citations, family size, opposition, and the value of patent rights. *Research Policy, 32,* 1343–1364.

Hausman, J., Hall, B. H., & Griliches, Z. (1984). Econometric models for count data with an application to patents R&D relationship. *Econometrica, 52,* 909–938.

Maddala, G. S. (1983). *Limited-dependent and qualitative variables in econometrics*. Cambridge: Cambridge University Press.

Shane, H., & Klock, M. (1997). The Relation Between Patent Citations and Tobins Q in the Semiconductor Industry, *Review of Quantitative Finance and Accounting, 9,* 131–146.

Trajtenberg, M. (1990). A penny for your quotes: Patent citation and the value of innovations. *Rand Journal of Economics, 21,* 172187.

Chapter 8
Conclusion

Abstract The existing economic literature lacks consensus on an appropriate method to quantify the strictness of environmental regulations. The objective of creating a stringency index for environmental regulations in this study was to understand the evolution of incrementally strict regulations to reduce vehicular emissions and fuel consumption. The empirical results provide preliminary evidence of an inducement effect of regulatory stringency to innovation activity as measured by weighted patent counts. The hypothesis that domestic regulatory stringency positively affects innovation was not rejected. Only in India and China, domestic stringency was found to stimulate domestic innovation. The finding reaffirmed that key emission norms implemented in the year 2000 and 2005 did induce innovation in both of these developing countries. These results support the Porter hypothesis that regulations can lead to more innovation. The results of this study are in line with Newell et al. (1999) who found that the direction of innovation was positive (inducement) for products covered under energy efficiency standards. The results also corroborate with findings of Popp (2006) who studied the effect of emission standards for NO_x and SO_2 on patenting in three countries including Germany between 1970 and 2000. He found that the innovators responded to environmental regulation of their home country but not to regulations of foreign countries. In the same year, Johnstone and Labonne (2009) also found that perceived stringency of environment regulation is a very strong driver of innovation. Hence, the results corroborate the argument that environment policy has a discernible (positive) impact on the direction of technological change and innovation. Based on the findings and background research of this study, some managerial and public policy implications are suggested below.

8.1 Managerial Implications

According to the expert commission setup by the German government to study technological innovation, competition and the patent system, electro-mobility was likely to become an important factor for stability and economic viability throughout

A. Bharadwaj, *Environmental Regulations and Innovation in Advanced Automobile Technologies*, SpringerBriefs in Economics,
https://doi.org/10.1007/978-981-10-6952-9_8

the world by 2020 (Harhoff 2004). Germany is one of the three world leaders in internal combustion engine technologies. Given the huge amount of investments already pumped into making the conventional engine more efficient, Germany is unlikely to fully embrace electric vehicles by 2020. Further, Germany, unlike Japan, is less likely to move to any non-conventional automotive technology on a commercially viable scale by 2020. With tightening emission norms, it will become more difficult for German car manufacturers to battle the environmental challenges and the inevitable transition to cleaner transport technologies such as battery-powered vehicles, electric cars, and long-range hybrids among others.

It was found that the views on investing in alternate propulsion systems are divergent. While one side believes that no significant technological breakthroughs are expected in the short to medium term, the other side believes that piecemeal transition approach to sustainable and cleaner transport is not only possible but is the best way to proceed. The latter argument is about the slow transition from conventional engines to hybrids and electrics to LNG- and hydrogen-powered vehicles.

This is undoubtedly a big window of opportunity for companies in the emerging economies since a big chunk of components (including complex technologies) are built by component manufactures instead of car manufacturers. When it comes to the R&D and patenting, the former not only has a bigger role to play, they also tend to have greater presence in countries other than their home country. The German government was accused in 2013 of siding with its two leading automobile manufacturers to block the revision of Europe's emission limit for carbon dioxide to 95 g/km. In this ongoing second phase of the Kyoto Protocol, it is important for the German automotive industry to actively focus on replacing (since they already have the capability to produce) the gas-guzzling vehicles to more environmentally friendly vehicles.

Technologically advanced automotive companies still need to do more in transferring (green) technologies. This is particularly true for countries such as China, Brazil, and India where scale of operations and market potential exceeds that of their home countries. It is clear that the domestic regulations in the host countries are not considered very strict for these companies because the compliant technologies are already at their disposal. Nevertheless, reliance on the argument "build it and they will come" is not likely to be successful in the long term. There are lessons to be learnt from some domestic companies (such as Tata in India) in order to understand the new market and to make useful partnerships. Foreign auto companies still need to differentiate between price-conscious consumers and value-conscious consumers in developing countries before bringing high value vehicles equipped with sophisticated (and clean) technologies.

Recently, the focus shifted to the importance of intellectual property (mainly, patents) that the developing countries, particularly India, were expected to give to all companies, domestic or foreign alike. This was built around the rhetoric that stronger intellectual property rights (mainly patents) are prerequisites of innovation and technology transfer. It is important to acknowledge the fact that transfer of enabling technical and non-technical know-how is as important as the transfer of technology. As long as the minimum standards of patent protection and entrepreneurship are assured in host countries under the TRIPS agreement, the foreign vendors of technology will find ways to get into these potentially lucrative markets. Countries like China and India need access to technologies (including energy efficient and low-carbon technologies) as much as foreign companies need access to these markets. The Weakness of the intellectual property regime in these countries hampers innovation by domestic companies. However, foreign companies, for the same reason, should not indulge in restricting output, overpricing or sidestepping local working requirements when entering new (emerging) markets.

Companies in developing countries that have sizable technological base should try to develop model R&D collaboration contracts, licensing contracts, and acquisition of useful patents. These companies, like in Europe and USA, should collaborate more with universities and research institutions to accelerate development and deployment of technologies in response to stringent regulations. This will get facilitated if there is a fast-track system for accelerated examination of green patent applications similar to what is already in place in Brazil. Foreign companies operating in Brazil and India for a long time tend to have a distinctive and strong IP strategy. This is particularly true for German companies and, additionally, Japanese companies in India.

Innovation collaboration in new (and green) automotive technologies is absolutely essential not only for the synergies emanating from the partnership, but also because it addresses a key problem of shortage of skills in some developing countries (such as in Brazil). This study found that regulations in Germany have an effect on innovation in the developing countries considered. But what the developing country companies can do (other than getting nudged by the regulator) is to make research partners for mutual benefit. In this context, the company could analyze the patterns and complementarities of technological specialization by potential partners in foreign countries. Indian and German companies have a high level of innovation collaboration, which is, in part, due to the size of the IT industry and the large pool of quality engineers available in India. This form of human capital is instrumental in tailoring foreign technologies to meet local needs with the help of well-designed employee training and skill enhancement programs.

8.2 Public Policy Implications

Environmental problems can be solved if the existing technologies are made available in the needed avenues and if the present regulatory system can provide the right incentives for the development of useful future technologies. Command and control type regulatory standards are more likely to give clear signals to the innovators to be able to effectively adhere to the requirements. Hence, instrument design is perhaps the most important aspect of a regulatory intervention. Another important aspect of an effective regulation found in this study was the appropriateness of timing and sense of commitment conveyed by the regulator.

An issue of importance to the European policy makers is that of free trade agreements between countries. It is well understood that bilateral trade policies affect industries in both nations and that an imbalance on any side has the ability to adversely affect the other. For example, emission norms and directives on fuel content will most assuredly affect American and Japanese car manufactures. With the rise of Chinese and Indian car companies, there is more competition to the German carmakers. A trade deal, not based on sound bilateral or multilateral discussions, is likely to hamper the prospects of growth of several players in the market. This problem was evident in the recently negotiated EU-India free trade agreement and the tariff disputes in the EU-China trade agreement.

In this study, there was a brief discussion on the "announcement effect" of regulations in the context of emission standards. It is often claimed by manufacturers in the industry that the time given to adapt to the new "rules" is inadequate for them. Now even if the life cycle of a typical automotive technology is long, the complaints raised by manufacturers about inadequacy of lead time is often a way to buy more time. This is not only to build new technologies or marketing channels but also to "push" into the market as many existing (less clean) technologies as possible.

A persistent unwillingness can also be because of the huge sunk cost in the form of R&D investments, but it can also be interpreted as repeated reluctance toward green laws. The developing countries can learn from the example of Europe's CO_2 emission laws that were passed in 2008 despite resistance from the industry. It is absolutely detrimental for local as well as global economy if policy makers in the developing world (particularly India and China) hold on to a "grow first, clean later" strategy. Developing countries, especially China, which is undergoing rapid industrialization, need to make their business environments more conducive for foreign automobile companies to operate. China currently requires all foreign car manufactures to forge alliances (JVs) with local companies to manufacture cars. India also "charges" this sort of "participation fee" from foreign companies to cash in on the emerging market frenzy. India, like Brazil, now requires local manufacturing of the product to safeguard the interest of the domestic companies.

While some would say it is the right policy (infant industry argument) to "safeguard" jobs, others would disagree on the ground that foreign companies not only bring with them new technologies, but they invest heavily in local infrastructure and "create" jobs. Unplanned and restrictive regulatory policies can add to these problems. As highlighted above, given the opportunity of taking the lead in future technologies, the developing countries need to adopt the right policies to facilitate the industry. Like Germany (and later India), Brazil (and China to some extent) needs to invest more in higher technical education to create a large human capital base. Brazil, India, and China should not become complacent in what they have achieved till now (although there is still a lot more to do) since there are several threshold economies, which will give tough competition to the BRIC countries in the near future. These include the other like-minded developing countries such as Mexico, Indonesia, South Korea, and Turkey (MIST), which share similar technological and economic strengths and opportunities.

A representative of a German company revealed that the industry, in his opinion, has gained from specific policies of the three emerging markets. According to him, infrastructural support in China, favorable government policies in Brazil, and availability of good engineers in India are important supply side factors. In another interview, it was pointed out that Indian and Brazilian auto industries consider China's industry to be a bigger threat than German, American, or Japanese industry. A common thread, in a big segment of the respective market in all three developing countries, is the preference for price and fuel economy of the vehicle than for a car with a small carbon footprint. However, there are significant differences too. The fundamental statistics of number of cars per thousand people is remarkably different. China was able to outpace every other economy in the past decade. However, China is now investing the most in cleaning it up at the same pace because China's tipping point of emissions may be approaching faster than previously thought.

Apart from regulatory steps and economic policies, China has witnessed a surge in patenting in the last decade unlike India or Brazil. India, on the other hand, needs to bridge the artificially created gap between petrol and diesel prices by decontrolling the latter. It should also cut down the excise duty on diesel cars. If boost in sales of medium and heavy commercial vehicles is seen as an indicator of economic growth, then imposing higher excise duties on this segment is counterintuitive. Increase in diesel price and giving more freedom to foreign investors will be like a tide that will have the potential to raise all (industrial) ships including the automotive sector. A lot still needs to be done in improving the fuel quality issues in India. Brazil has done relatively well in adopting the right policies and regulations including timely adoption of emission norms. However, it needs to create a stronger base for ancillary companies to facilitate entry and expansion of bigger manufacturers (OEMs). If anthropogenic climate change is happening because of (over) use or misuse of technologies, then the answer also lies, in part at least, in the development, dissemination, and deployment of green technologies. All actors in the welfare chain, including the regulator and the innovator, need to play their respective roles to facilitate this.

8.3 Caveats and Future Research

This study has discussed the issue of green innovation and regulation in a developing country context that was not covered well in the existing literature. However, the results suffer from two main issues. First, the innovation activity may well be influencing regulation and its strictness. This is particularly true in the competitive automotive industry in which practices need to have an international conformity. This feedback effect or reverse causality was not taken into consideration, and thus, the strength of the results is less clear. Second, the study only considered one technology pioneer (German) and did not include USA and Japan, which are the other two prominent countries in the automotive business. Including only Germany, even though it is the leader in automotive technologies in Europe, compromises the external validity of the results. On the other hand, only three developing countries were chosen. Although support for the Porter hypothesis was found, the results lack robustness because of exclusion of other developing countries due to inadequate yearly data at the technology level. Further research is therefore necessary given the importance of the increasingly converging regulations across countries. The use of important determinants of technology adoption and regulatory strictness across a larger cross-section of countries to replicate the findings is a topic for future research.

References

Harhoff, D. (2004). Innovationen und Wettbewerbspolitik - Anstzezurkonomis- chenAnalyse des Patensystems, Vortragbei der Jubilumsveranstaltung, 30 Jahre Monopolkommission, Berlin.

Johnstone, N., & Labonne, J. (2009). Environmental policy, management and R&D. *OECD Economic Studies, 1*.

Popp, D. (2006). International innovation and diffusion of air pollution control technologies: The effects of NO_x and SO_2 regulation in the US, Japan, and Germany. *Journal of Environmental Economics and Management, 51*(1), 46–71.

Newell, R.G., Jaffe, A. B., & Stavins, R. N. (1999). The Induced Innovation Hypothesis and Energy-Saving Technological Change. *The Quarterly Journal of Economics 114*(3), 941–975

MIX
Papier aus verantwortungsvollen Quellen
Paper from responsible sources
FSC® C105338

If you have any concerns about our products,
you can contact us on
ProductSafety@springernature.com

In case Publisher is established outside the EU,
the EU authorized representative is:
Springer Nature Customer Service Center GmbH
Europaplatz 3, 69115 Heidelberg, Germany

Printed by Libri Plureos GmbH
in Hamburg, Germany